CW00552849

NEVER NOT WORKING

NEVER NOT WORKING

Why the Always—On Culture
Is Bad for Business—
and How to Fix It

MALISSA CLARK

Harvard Business Review Press
Boston, Massachusetts

Printed in the United Kingdom by TJ Books Limited, Padstow, Cornwall

10 9 8 7 6 5 4 3 2

Library of Congress Cataloging-in-Publication Data

Names: Clark, Malissa, author.
Title: Never not working : why the always-on culture is bad for business, and how to fix it / Malissa Clark.
Description: Boston, Massachusetts : Harvard Business Review Press, [2023] | Includes index.
Identifiers: LCCN 2023033138 (print) | LCCN 2023033139 (ebook) | ISBN 9781647825096 (hardcover) | ISBN 9781647825102 (epub)
Subjects: LCSH: Workaholism. | Workaholics. | Mental fatigue. | Psychology, Industrial. | Success in business.
Classification: LCC RC569.5.W67 C53 2023 (print) | LCC RC569.5.W67 (ebook) | DDC 616.85/2--dc23/eng/20230921
LC record available at https://lccn.loc.gov/2023033138
LC ebook record available at https://lccn.loc.gov/2023033139

ISBN: 978-1-64782-509-6
eISBN: 978-1-64782-510-2

The paper used in this publication meets the requirements of the American National Standard for Permanence of Paper for Publications and Documents in Libraries and Archives Z39.48-1992.

For Alex and Evan:
I love you.
—Mom

CONTENTS

NEVER NOT
WORKING

The Age of Overwork

From a young age, Marina felt like she was wasting time if she wasn't actively *doing* something. By high school, she had learned how to fill all her hours—first with school, then with soccer or track after school, then homework until midnight. She also got a job at an ice cream shop and, later, a pizza place. To build her academic résumé, she added student council, class vice president, school board student representative, and vice president of the Key Club. She topped it off with volunteering at Big Brothers Big Sisters.

College demanded more studying and fewer sports, but Marina also worked thirty hours per week on top of her full class load. When summer came, she took a job selling books door-to-door, working eighty-hour weeks and receiving awards for her time put in.

This success led to an intense sales job that consumed her until she decided she also wanted to get a PhD. In academia, Marina managed to repeat the pattern, putting in extreme hours and participating in as many committees and programs as she could until she reached the top and received her doctorate and a professorship.

All along, Marina knew she was overworking but didn't seem to know how to stop. If she was being honest, she didn't *want* to stop. She lived off the adrenaline and always felt dread when she thought about not having enough to do.

Marina was a workaholic. I know this because I have made it my life's work to study overwork and its effects on people and organizations. I have dedicated myself to learning why and how our culture has evolved to encourage overwork and why it's becoming a bigger, more pervasive problem than ever. This book is dedicated to that exploration and to sharing the ways we can fight back against workaholism.

I also know this because I'm Marina.

The biographical details I just shared are mine, Malissa's. I'm not that person anymore. I've worked hard to control my workaholic tendencies. And now, I want to share what I've learned to overcome it.

Why Now?

Why am I writing this book now? The truth is, it's long overdue. I've known what the data says for some time. I've experienced the effects of being an overworker, and I've spoken with and worked with so many others who've also experienced them. I could have written this book a couple of years ago. But there was that global pandemic; also, I'm not sure if the world was ready to hear the message about the devastating effects of workaholism on ourselves and others back then. I'm hopeful that now is finally a time when people might be open to *really* hearing the facts and data about overwork and why it needs to be addressed. STAT.

You may have related to Marina's (my) story. It's not surprising, given that this sort of hustle culture has been ingrained in us from a young age and is ingraining itself deeply in the emerging generation that has never known a world without constant connection and on-demand service—two hallmarks of hustle culture. We learn from our first years that if you work hard enough, you can achieve anything you want. The implicit message there is that if you did not meet your childhood goals, then maybe you didn't work hard enough or put enough effort toward them. As adults, we have adopted "busy" as a status symbol, lest someone think we are not devoted to our work. Think about the question you hear daily: "How are you?" What's the common answer, "Relaxed and not thinking about work, actually" or "Crazy busy!"

Technology tethers us to our work through smartphones and "productivity" apps such as Slack and Teams, and the majority of workers regularly check their email on their smartphones, which never leave our side, even after work hours or on vacation. The rise in remote work means work and family spheres are no longer separate, blurring the boundaries between work and home. Or as Andrew Barnes, entrepreneur and cofounder of 4 Day Week Global, put it to me, "We're not working from home, we're sleeping in the office."[1] This is our new world of work.

I'm not saying that hard work is bad. Or that all hard work is workaholism. I'm saying that we need this book now because our relationship with work is becoming increasingly unhealthy. Levels of burnout and stress are at all-time highs. Even before the pandemic, the World Health Organization called stress the "health epidemic of the 21st century."[2] What is a major source of that stress? Our jobs. Covid-19 exacerbated this problem. During the pandemic, workdays became longer—in the United States, the average workday is now three hours longer; and in the United Kingdom, France, Canada, and Spain, it's two hours longer.[3] But more than that, we have gotten used to working outside traditional work hours. Microsoft has conducted several studies analyzing keystroke data and use of its collaboration software Teams chat feature. Results reveal two disturbing trends: compared with prepandemic, during Covid, (1) we were much more likely to work in the evenings, typically in the hours before bedtime, in what has been dubbed the "triple peak day" and (2) the number of work messages sent and received on the weekends increased by 200 percent.[4]

Now, three years later, the patterns that emerged in a crisis have been normalized. We have gotten used to them in just the same way people may develop a bad habit. What's even worse is that this increased workload, connectivity to work, and altered communication patterns have been tacked on to our existing schedules, meaning we are working longer and staying more tethered to work than ever before.

This is happening everywhere, too. It's not just an American problem. Workaholism has been shown to be a problem all around the world. What *is* uniquely American is the fact that the United States is the *only* industrialized nation to offer zero days of paid maternity/paternity leave, and the only country in the OECD to offer zero days of paid leave at the federal level.[5] Even in Japan, also known for its workaholic culture, the federal government mandates that workers get a minimum of ten paid days of annual leave. In other words, workaholism in the United States is not entirely a cultural phenomenon; it's structurally reinforced and encouraged.

In other parts of the world, particularly in Europe, there are encouraging signs that overwork is given the consideration it deserves. For example, in 2017 the French government implemented a "right to disconnect" law, which is a legal requirement for employers with fifty-plus employees to set out hours when staff are not required to send or answer emails. Since then, other European countries, including Italy, Belgium, Spain, and Ireland, have implemented similar laws.[6] And then there's Iceland, which recently participated in a four-day week trial with *resounding* success: workers went from a forty-hour schedule to a thirty-five- or thirty-six-hour schedule, employees were happier, and organizations reported no loss in productivity—some even reported *increased* productivity.[7]

Movements such as 4 Day Week Global continue to build momentum across the world, and the data is overwhelmingly positive.[8] Companies are taking employee mental health more seriously than ever before.[9] New technologies such as AI will further improve our efficiency and productivity, allowing us to accomplish tasks in less time. Leaders and organizations have a plethora of high-quality tools and resources at their fingertips to assess and improve worker well-being in their organizations.[10] We do not need to work ourselves literally to death; there is another way.

And we *have* to choose that other way. That's why I'm writing this book now. To help you make that choice, to show you that, yes, you can choose balance over work obsession, and to give you some practical approaches for doing that.

A Broader Approach

When I set out to understand overwork, I was surprised to learn just how much academic research already existed on the topic. At the same time, it was of varying quality and much of it was not being communicated to anyone outside of academia. It was as if researchers had discovered a new infection but hadn't thought to mention their discovery to the infected. Why, I thought, are we not applying these findings to a public that is so clearly overworked and burning out? We knew in academia that overwork was happening; we knew that it carried massive costs to people and to organizations and communities. Yet little was being done. I wanted to change that.

What's more, I found that the books published on the topic were almost exclusively devoted to individuals and focused on individual strategies for combating workaholism. Self-help, if you will. I wanted to take a broader approach, because my research was uncovering a systemic problem driven not just by people like me with workaholic tendencies, but by the norms and expectations and, yes, even rules set by organizations and by society itself. This felt like an important piece of the puzzle that was missing. Just as we can't solve employee burnout by focusing only on self-care, we can't address the negative effects of workaholism without first addressing the places demanding an always-available, work-first talent pool.

This book is that broader approach. In addition to helping individuals recognize the signs of workaholism in themselves and others, it highlights several places you could look to understand potential leverage points for organizational change, regardless of whether you identify as a workaholic. What are the red flags for spotting whether an employee or supervisor is a workaholic? What are companies doing wrong? What are they doing right? Is your organization promoting well-being initiatives—often with the best of intentions—but simultaneously sending mixed signals to employees about what is valued and rewarded?

Perhaps most important to organizations, I arm you with hard data about the costs of workaholism to both individuals and companies. So often in my work, I meet resistance to this message that work-above-all is deeply inefficient and costly. Some people point to individuals as the problem (just as we used to blame individuals solely for problems like alcoholism, until we evolved to understand all the forces at play). Others suggest that what I'm researching is interesting but not applicable to them. They see only positive results from their hard-charging culture.

But I know from the research and the data that those results don't last and come at a cost. A real, human cost. I hope this book is a lever for people who want to change their culture with the means to convince other, more skeptical people they work with that they *need* to make this change.

How This Book Works

I'll proceed simply, first by looking at the individual, then the organization.

In chapter 1, "Workaholism Myths and Realities," I'll set a working definition of the affliction and push back on some common misconceptions about workaholism that limit our full understanding of how insidious it can be. I challenge the notion that workaholism is not really that big a deal and is mostly a problem isolated to a few industries or occupations. I also challenge the notion that workaholism is a good thing—that workaholics are the best workers and that there are some good types of workaholics.

In chapter 2, "A Portrait of the Modern Workaholic," you'll learn about many of the characteristic of overworkers, including extreme examples. I dig a little deeper into the science behind why workaholism is so detrimental. Crucially, this portrait also includes how this affliction affects the people *around* the workaholic, and I share personal stories of loved ones of workaholics. Finally, I spend more time talking about (and debunking) the idea that workaholism is related to better performance.

Chapter 3, "Kicking the Habit," provides you with methods for raising awareness of workaholic tendencies in yourself or others and six strategies for counteracting those tendencies. Anyone who has found themselves ruminating about work at unwanted times or feeling deep guilt for not working will want to start implementing some of these practical strategies right away.

Chapter 4, "Are You an Enabler?" pivots toward the organizational drivers of always-on workaholic cultures. I talk about the deeply rooted cultural drivers of workaholism and the organizational signals, policies, and practices that perpetuate it. Anyone who manages other people or who is trying to understand the complex intermixing of personal and organizational factors driving workaholism will find surprising and valuable insights here.

Finally, in chapter 5, "Fixing Your Culture of Overwork," I provide actionable steps that you can take in your organization to assess, plan, and execute changes that will, over time and with effort, break down your workaholic cultural enablers.

.   .   .

All of this is buffered by research, both qualitative and quantitative. As an academic, I began searching for answers to the questions brought on by overwork by diving into the scholarly research and conducting my own research. But I didn't stop there. I also reviewed the popular press books on the subject and, with my invaluable research team, interviewed close to a hundred individuals who either struggle with workaholism, are partner to a workaholic, study the topic, or manage organizations and are dedicated to finding a better balance between work and life.

Throughout this book, you will hear their stories—firsthand experiences of the impacts of workaholism and overwork culture—and you will hear from those who've escaped the clutches of their own obsession with work. You will hear from individuals in all ranks of organizations, working all kinds of jobs, from a variety of cultures. You may see yourself reflected in some of these stories, or they may remind you of someone you know. I am grateful for the time each of them took to share their stories, and to Workaholics Anonymous for their assistance reaching out to their members. The stories I heard were often heart-wrenching, and sometimes I felt that the problem was simply too big, too insidious, and too pervasive for me to make a difference. I wondered if change was possible. However, I also heard enough inspiring stories of recovery and change that I felt hope and was reminded why this book is necessary. In some cases, I've used pseudonyms and replaced personal details to protect the individuals who so graciously helped me.

My goal with this book is to translate what we have learned through decades of research about workaholism and overwork culture to the people who have the ability and capacity to make actionable changes to benefit workers and themselves. (So often, those in a position to make change discover they are workaholics themselves, unknowingly modeling the very behavior that leads to so many problems in the workforce.)

Change will be hard, and there is no simple, one-size-fits-all approach, but you can do it. You will hear from both individuals and organizations that have made substantive changes to their culture and seen productivity *gains*, not losses, and *higher* engagement, not lower.

If you are reading this book, this suggests to me that you and your organization are willing to change and face these tough questions. This is the first step. Congratulations. Let's get started.

CHAPTER 1

Workaholism Myths and Realities

Let's start with some data. On average, people work fewer hours than ever.[1] In countries with higher GDP, hours worked have declined the most. Also, in those countries, people on average earn more money than ever and therefore require fewer hours to live comfortably.[2] According to the late sociologist John Robinson, also known as "Father Time" for his extensive research on time use, most people have around forty hours of free time per week—that's about a quarter of all time in the week and, assuming eight hours of sleep, free time is 36 percent of waking hours.[3] Recently, companies around the world have implemented a four-day work-week with positive results: productivity gains were matched by employee satisfaction gains.[4]

So, why am I writing a book about workaholism? From these statistics, it might seem that it's becoming *less* of a problem, not more. Well, let's add some more data: workaholism is on the rise around the world. Today, almost half of US workers would classify themselves as workaholics.[5] According to a 2019 *Forbes* survey, that percentage is even higher for Millennials —66 percent. In addition, 70 percent of the Millennials in the survey admitted to working most weekends, two-thirds admitted to working even when they were sick, and one-third admitted to working while sitting on the toilet.[6] In 2018, 55 percent of Americans failed to use all of their paid time off, leaving 768 million vacation days on the table.[7] This work fixation is expensive. Costs associated with the inevitable burnout and related health problems that accompany overwork are increased risk of metabolic syndrome, elevated blood pressure, greater susceptibility to autoimmune illnesses, poor sleep, poor physical and mental health, increased job stress and work-family conflict, and decreased job and family satisfaction.[8]

Before we square these seemingly contradictory paragraphs, it's important to remember that these are averages; the distribution of these trends is anything but even. Some people are working more and making less, and the systemic issues that have led to their being left out of the broader trend of higher pay and more free time must be addressed. For some, overwork isn't an affliction; it's a necessity to make ends meet, and that problem cannot be ignored, though it's not my primary focus.

At the same time, it seems strange that on average people work less and make more, yet at the same time are more likely to identify as workaholics. If you were an HR leader, you could dismiss this as so much empty complaining by some workers. It may be tempting to throw up your hands and ask, *What else do you want?* And you may think there's no real return on assessing and mitigating workaholism in your organization. That would be a mistake. For just as workaholism is problematic for the workers, it's expensive to organizations, too. Costs include higher turnover and absenteeism, rising health-care costs given the negative physical and mental toll on workers, and decreased business growth as well as the less quantifiable outcomes that arise when the workforce is unengaged, unhappy, exhausted, and burned out.[9]

The fundamental disconnect here is that most of us—workers or leaders or HR departments—have an erroneous sense of what workaholism is. Usually, we think it's directly correlated with *how much* we work. We tally hours and decide that too many hours on the job—sixty a week? Eighty? A hundred?—turn one into a workaholic.

Nope. It turns out that work hours are *not* a strong predictor of workaholism.[10] They don't tell the full story, and they certainly don't help you identify and mitigate the problem—which you need to do. That's why those two paragraphs of data can coexist. Workaholism is about so much more than just a quantity of hours at work.

Sure, work hours may an obvious sign of workaholism, but it's more than that. Workaholism also involves that feeling in the pit of your stomach that you *can't* rest, that you *ought to* be working all the time. Workaholism also involves feeling *guilty* and *anxious* when you are not working. It's the fact that even if you are not physically doing work, you are thinking about that email you should send, mulling over that upcoming work project, or ruminating about something that happened at work that day. It's living with the fear of losing something—status, money, the job itself—if you're not working.

Whether you're the one suffering or you're someone who's managing a group of workaholics, this problem needs to be addressed, because, having researched this phenomenon for more than fifteen years, I can tell you that the effects of workaholism are worse than you think—both physically and socially—for people, teams, and organizations.

Even if you do not identify as a workaholic, you are negatively affected by the workaholic(s) around you, whether it is your spouse, boss, coworkers, or friends. Perhaps you are shouldering more than your fair share of domestic responsibilities because your partner is a workaholic. Or you have a boss who constantly texts (and expects

Myth: Workaholics are the ideal workers

Throughout this chapter, I'll bust common workaholism myths. Here is the first one: the myth of the *ideal worker*—someone who wholly devotes themselves to work above all else, and who persists despite plenty of evidence that the ideal worker doesn't exist and isn't a good model. The workaholic strives to embody the ideal worker prototype—perfectly efficient human capital to be deployed and used to its fullest extent. But for all the reasons outlined in this chapter, and more that will come throughout the rest of this book, it doesn't work. It will backfire every time.

a response) after hours, no matter the time or day. Maybe you have a coworker who sets unrealistic standards for your team based on their idea—not yours—of how connected to work you should be. It could be that your best friend has drifted from you because they only ever want to talk about work when you get together, and they get irritated or disconnected talking about anything else. There are children who suffer due to a parent's fixation on their work, and their insistence that the fixation is the very thing providing the child with opportunities in life.

These are only some of the real problems I've observed in my research. The entire scope of the negative effect of obsession with work are far-reaching and, in a few cases, even deadly. It's so common that some languages even have a word for it. In Japan, the word is *karoshi*—which translates roughly to "death from overwork." In China, the term is *guolaosi*. Estimates for rates of *guolaosi* in China are staggering, with some reports placing it as high as over a million workers each year.[11] In chapter 3, I'll go into more detail about personal stories of how workaholism affects people's lives (not just the workaholic's, but of those around them). But for now, it's important to know two things about the effects of workaholism: One, it leads to serious, negative physical and mental effects. And two, people usually believe they themselves are immune to those effects, even if others aren't, and that they can manage them, even if others can't. But they are fooling themselves. The science doesn't lie.

We know that workaholics are at greater risk of negative health events, including cardiovascular disease, sleep problems, and elevated blood pressure.[12] I've spoken with individuals who have experienced *more than one* heart attack while working. Typically, just one heart attack is not enough to get workaholics to try to change, believe it or not. Every single workaholic I interviewed for this book has faced a health issue that is directly or indirectly tied to their overwork.

Workaholics are also much more likely than the average worker to experience severe burnout, which involves overwhelming exhaustion, feelings of cynicism and detachment from the job, and a sense of lack of accomplishment.[13] I've found that workaholics are particularly likely to experience the exhaustion component.[14] It's not hard to draw a line from these effects to poor effects for the organization.

We may work less, yes. But the problem is not the hours on the job; it's that our relationship to work and its meaning to us is becoming increasingly unhealthy. If we're going to fix it, we need to understand clearly what we are and are not dealing with here.

Workaholism Is *Not . . .*

To know what workaholism is beyond some arbitrary number of hours worked, first we need to understand what it is *not*.

It's Not a Clinical Condition

It's easy to see that the term *workaholism* (which, I know, isn't great) derives from the common trope of adding *-aholic* to a noun to describe any sort of obsession—from mild, like chocolate or shopping, to true compulsions.

Obviously, the *-ism* of workaholism makes the noun become about the condition rather than the person. It's a bit more awkward sounding, but it's become the term of art and it's what we'll most commonly use to describe the problem. It was not coined in the same vein as, say, *chocoholic* or *shopaholic*, which are generally considered playful deployments of the suffix. Rather it's meant to evoke the term *alcoholism* because workaholism shares similarities with behavioral disorders such as that and with gambling addiction, and it is a phenomenon that is studied deeply and well understood.

But a doctor can't clinically diagnose it like those other conditions because it is not in the DSM—the *Diagnostic and Statistical Manual of Mental Disorders*. The DSM is the guidebook used by professionals to provide an official diagnosis of a disorder or mental illness, and disorders get added or removed from it through a rather involved and lengthy process. Even though workaholism meets many of the relevant clinical criteria for inclusion in the DSM, including having a negative impact on the individual and their relationships and unsuccessful attempts to reduce the activity, I do not anticipate that it will ever make it into the manual. As one clinical psychologist and former workaholic whom I interviewed noted, because it is so pervasive, if workaholism or work addiction were added to the DSM, then a giant swath of the population would instantly be classified as having a clinical condition. Workaholism, in other words, is the only socially acceptable—dare I say, respected—addiction.

The term *workaholism* was originally coined by pastor and psychologist Wayne Oates in his 1971 book *Confessions of a Workaholic*, in which he admits to being a workaholic himself. There are many related terms floating around out there, including *work addiction* and *overwork*. On social media, you might see the hashtags #toxicproductivity, #workmartyr, or #hustleculture. I think these all fundamentally get at the same thing, but for the sake of clarity and consistency, throughout this book I am going to mostly use the terms *workaholism* and *workaholic* and occasionally use terms like *overwork* and its derivatives.

It's Not Just Working Long Hours

Research studies show clear differences between work hours and workaholism.[15] It would be incorrect to assume that every employee working long hours is a workaholic. There are a variety of reasons someone might work long hours: Financial demands for which extra hours bring much-needed family income. A busy season that makes long hours unavoidable, albeit temporary. Or a demanding boss who requires extra hours.

Yes, working long work hours is certainly often a part of being a workaholic. But just knowing that a person works all the time isn't enough to identify workaholism. It's only one signal. I established this earlier, I know, but I think it's worth repeating here, if for no other reason than to remove this sticky assumption from our minds.

It's Not the Same Thing as Work Engagement

There are many definitions of work engagement, but the most common and most well-accepted ones focus on a few core attributes:

- Feeling energy and resilience

- Showing enthusiasm and commitment

- Demonstrating immersion or absorption in work

Myth: There are "good" types of workaholics

Many efforts have been made to create workaholic typologies identifying different varieties of workaholics, including so-called good ones. The most common "good" type of workaholic is the *enthusiastic workaholic* or the *engaged workaholic*. This refers to people who embody all the qualities of workaholism but also love what they do. The tiny kernel of truth is that loving your work may provide a slight buffer from the most negative outcomes of workaholism; for example, researchers Lieke ten Brummelhuis and Nancy Rothbard compared engaged workaholics to nonengaged workaholics and found that nonengaged workaholics' risk of metabolic syndrome was 4.2 percent higher.[a] However, regardless of levels of work engagement, all the workaholics in their study had higher depressive feelings, sleep problems, and health complaints, and a higher need for recovery than non-workaholics. Other research flat-out debunks this

Many of these same descriptors begin to get at some of the ways workaholics feel about work, too, just to an unhealthy degree. Also, it's the vector of those feelings that is different for a workaholic than for others. For example, the workaholic demonstrates immersion through fear or anxiety of being *not* immersed, not necessarily through genuine interest in the work.

Given how wonderful the idea of engagement sounds in some cases, workaholism is celebrated as a kind of pure form of engagement with work. A workaholic is someone who loves what they myth of the engaged workaholic as a positive form of workaholism. For example, Nicolas Gillet and colleagues examined the combined effects of workaholism and work engagement in a series of three independent studies. They found that *any positive effects of work engagement were effectively eliminated if the individual was also a workaholic.*[b] Thus, loving your work may provide, at best, slightly less deleterious outcomes, but most likely, the truth is that any benefits of loving your work are essentially washed out by your work compulsion—particularly if one looks at the long-term risks of workaholism. Even the most enthusiastic workaholic will experience negative outcomes in the long run.

a. Lieke ten Brummelhuis and Nancy P. Rothbard, "How Being a Workaholic Differs from Working Long Hours—and Why That Matters for Your Health," hbr.org, March 22, 2018, https://hbr.org /2018/03/how-being-a-workaholic-differs-from-working-long -hours-and-why-that-matters-for-your-health.

b. Nicolas Gillet et al., "Investigating the Combined Effects of Workaholism and Work Engagement: A Substantive-Methodological Synergy of Variable-Centered and Person-Centered Methodologies," *Journal of Vocational Behavior* 109 (2018): 54–77 https://doi .org/10.1016/j.jvb.2018.09.006.

do so much that it becomes their entire world. Given this idea, we often see the term used with a positive connotation, often as a humble brag:[16] *I was such a workaholic this weekend!* Or, *My schedule is so packed I didn't even have time to eat lunch.* Or, *I could have gone to the beach today, but instead I worked on my extra project I took on at work.*

The most obvious (to others) reason that engagement and workaholism are conflated is that individuals who are highly engaged in their work often are hyperfocused on it, just as many workaholics are. Engagement and workaholism can look similar.

Take Sam, for example. Every day, Sam drops his kids off at school at 8:15 and heads directly to the office. At work, his behavior is predictable. He's either intently working at his desk or walking and talking to clients on the phone. He doesn't join his colleagues for lunch because he gets into a "flow" and doesn't want to break his concentration. Occasionally, he'll stop by a happy hour. Everyone knows that Sam is easily accessible after hours by phone or text to answer a quick question, and many have received communication from him at extreme hours.

Is Sam a workaholic? Maybe. Is Sam an engaged worker? Also, maybe. Without knowing what is under the surface—what's *inside Sam*—it is almost impossible to tell. And in fact, Sam could be both engaged with his work and a workaholic. We shouldn't think of these two phenomena as two extreme ends of a spectrum, but rather twin spectrums that exist in parallel. Imagine two meters, both set low to high. The first is engagement, the second workaholism. Someone who deeply enjoys their work will skew right on the first meter. And if they take family vacations, have good friends, enjoy hobbies, and are generally pleasant to be around, they'll be low on the second meter. Conversely, someone who is fanatically focused on getting work done out of fear they will be fired and who has drifted from all friends, possibly isn't available to their kids, and complains constantly about work will be low on engagement and high on workaholism. Then of course, there's the person who is wedded to their work but to the detriment of other relationships and their physical health, who would be high on both meters. That's the engaged workaholic.

So if the engaged worker and the workaholic can exist in parallel like this, how do you distinguish between the two? Two ways: locate where the energy is being spent, and understand the motivation to work.

Where is the energy being spent? Crucially, engagement is thought of as what's achieved *while working*—a state of being excited and vigorously absorbed in one's work. It could be anything from working on a national expansion strategy for your startup company to interacting with a creative team to launch a new product. It could be helping customers purchase their dream product or achieve some major goal or helping a customer identify and implement new workplace practices that improve their employees' job satisfaction. Any of these and many more can be energizing for employees. But notice too that all of these activities are centered on what is done within the boundaries of their job.

On the other hand, much of what defines workaholism occurs outside of those work boundaries—tinkering with your work project instead of going to the beach, constantly taking work calls when you're with your family, having obsessive thoughts about a customer interaction that's over and done with, or turning conversations with friends into stories about your work. When the energy of work permeates every aspect of your life, that suggests workaholism. Engaged workers have a much easier time turning off work (mentally and physically) at the appropriate time, whereas workaholics cannot.

What's the motivation to work? An even more critical differentiator between the engagement and workaholism is the motivation behind work. It helps to know *why* a person is working as much and as hard as they do and *why* work is such a central part of that person's life. Psychologists have discovered that a key driver of employee engagement is *intrinsic* motivation, which is when someone does something because they love it. According to self-determination theory, intrinsic motivation is a positive motivational state that is beneficial because the person is engaging in an

Myth: Workaholism is limited to certain occupations

If you paid me every time someone told me, "Oh, this is such a problem in the [fill in the blank] industry, not mine," I would be able to take my family on some pretty fancy vacations. Workaholism is widespread across all industries and most occupations: law, medicine, sales, marketing, consulting, IT, academia, journalism, retail, manufacturing, and many, many more. I've interviewed workaholics from all over the world and from almost every occupation you can imagine, and what strikes me is that no matter how distinct their jobs or industries, their stories are remarkably similar. The outcomes are the same.

activity of their own volition.[17] When individuals are the ones in control of what they choose to do and choose not to do, they are able to meet an innate psychological need. And when we are able to meet our psychological needs, we are happier, healthier, and more productive.

But there is another type of motivation that drives people to work a lot or put work at the center of their lives: *introjected* motivation. This is when individuals are engaging in an activity based on extrinsic pressures that they partially internalize. External pressures can be any motivating force that comes from outside: a salary, an insistent boss, pressure from a parent or peers. But even if they start as external pressure, over time, they become something we feel we need to maintain. They *feel* intrinsic to us even if they're not.

For a workaholic, this internalized pressure can stem from notions about work that we have adopted and that are perpetuated societally.

When someone grows up constantly being told and shown that their worth and identity are directly tied to work, high salaries, successful promotions, external demonstrations of wealth (e.g., a big house), and so on, these values, which come from the outside, are partially internalized and reinforced throughout their life. And by the time they are a working adult, their long hours are intertwined with the idea that they must work constantly in order to feel worthy.[18]

Psychologist Toon Taris and his colleagues describe this difference as the "push" and "pull" of work.[19] Whereas work engagement involves a pull to work—a desire to work because of intrinsic motivation—workaholism involves a push to work because of internalized pressures that came from outside that one *ought* to be working. And again, this is not an either/or scenario. You can experience both simultaneously.

. . .

One final point about workaholism. I alluded to this when discussing the interplay of work engagement and workaholism as two independent meters, but I want to make sure I bring this point home. Workaholism, just like *any other* aspect of our personality or work style, exists on a continuum. It's not as cut-and-dried as "You either are or aren't a workaholic." This is why you will see me use the term *workaholic tendencies* throughout the book. You might have a few workaholic tendencies, so you might relate to some of the things I discuss, but not all of them. Or you might have a lot of workaholic tendencies, so you might relate to each of the components of workaholism. Or you might not have any of these tendencies at all. The point is, there is nuance that I am oversimplifying for the sake of explaining the phenomenon at a high level. Just keep in mind that when I talk about links between workaholism

Myth: Workaholics are more productive

Maybe you're a leader thinking, *Yeah—they may not be the healthiest person, but I'm getting so much out of them, I'll look the other way.* No. My meta-analysis, which looked at the results of all studies examining the relationship between workaholism and performance, found no evidence that workaholism equates with added productivity or better performance. What my colleagues and I found is that:

- Workaholics overextend themselves and don't leave time to recover their spent resources.

- Workaholics tend to work more, not smarter.

- Workaholics often find work that's not necessary, to feed their inner compulsion.

- Workaholics can be difficult teammates and bosses, often setting unrealistic timelines for projects and causing unnecessary stress for others.

- Workaholics are more likely to engage in counterproductive work behaviors that harm the organization.

and outcomes, just because you may not relate to being a full-blown workaholic, it doesn't mean you aren't at an increased risk of negative outcomes of overwork compared with people who do not have any of these tendencies. Another way to think about it is this: people who smoke just a few cigarettes a day are still considered "smokers" and are still susceptible to negative health effects, but it is also reasonable to assume that people who smoke two packs of cigarettes a day are at an increased risk.

Studies looking specifically at the cause-and-effect relationship between workaholism and job performance found no support for the idea that workaholism positively affects future job performance; in fact, their results suggest the opposite—that our job performance may actually impact future levels of workaholism.[a] The research also shows that workaholism predicts *decreases* in work engagement over time.[b] In another study, researchers found that managers could not tell the difference between those who were workaholics and those who only *pretended* to be workaholics to align with organizational expectations—both groups received similar performance evaluations.[c]

a. Xiaohong Xu et al., "Does Working Hard Really Pay Off? Testing the Temporal Ordering between Workaholism and Job Performance," *Journal of Occupational and Organizational Psychology* (May 2023): 1–21, https://doi.org/10.1111/joop.12441.

b. István Tóth-Kiraly et al., "A Longitudinal Perspective on the Associations between Work Engagement and Workaholism," *Work and Stress* 35, no. 1 (2021): 27–56, https://doi.org/10.1080/02678373.2020.1801888.

c. Erin Reid, "Why Some Men Pretend to Work 80-Hour Weeks," hbr.org, April 28, 2015, https://hbr.org/2015/04/why-some-men-pretend-to-work-80-hour-weeks; "Are the Workaholics You Know Just Faking It?" hbr.org video, October 26, 2015, https://hbr.org/video/4578695106001/are-the-workaholics-you-know-just-faking-it.

Workaholism Is . . .

Even in disqualifying some aspects of what people may think workaholism is not, we start to see what it is. But to really understand it, we need a full working definition. Through studying workaholism over the past decade and conducting interviews with workaholics and the people around them, I've developed a framework for defining and understanding workaholism.

There are four main components of workaholism: behavioral, motivational, cognitive, and emotional. Each is necessary to identify it, but none is sufficient by itself to consider someone a workaholic.

Behavioral: Excessive Working

This is the most obvious aspect of workaholism—workaholics work well beyond what is required and expected. No matter the job's requirements, the workaholic will always do *more*. Workaholics also tend to struggle with delegation, which adds to their excessive effort. They may have crafted a story in their mind that their project will fall apart if they step away, or that they are the only person who can get something right. They may also have internalized the idea of the lone hero—that they will be justly rewarded for being the person who does the most. As you might imagine, this lack of delegation has downstream consequences for their ability to be a good teammate and leader. Workaholics can also be performative about their excessive working, making it known in both subtle and obvious ways that they are overextended, "flat out," or "drowning in work," bragging about their endurance and contributions while at the same time scoffing at anyone who clocks fewer hours than they do or chooses something other than work to focus on.

Workaholics work even when they shouldn't—for example, when they are sick or injured. This is called *presenteeism*, which has been shown to reduce individual productivity by one-third or more. Presenteeism is, in fact, more costly to organizations than absenteeism.[20] Rewarding workaholics by recognizing their over-devotion, then, costs the company. It costs the workers, too. Workaholics are notoriously bad at making time for important doctor appointments, with the rationale that they simply don't have the time. Throughout the book, you will hear stories of people who have

Myth: Men are more likely than women to be workaholics

The stereotypical workaholic is indeed a man. Perhaps when you've been reading this chapter, you've been picturing a type A man without even realizing it. Someone like Skip, a seventy-three-year-old business owner and author who at times has held two full-time jobs simultaneously. Currently, Skip works seven days a week, and when I asked him when he was planning on retiring, he said, "Never." Skip represents a cultural norm—the expectation for a man to be the ideal worker, devoted to his work above all else. As a society, we remain fiercely stuck with the traditional gender roles of the man as the provider and the woman as the caregiver. Thus, it's more socially acceptable for men to overwork, especially if they have a partner at home tending to the family.

But in fact, men and women are equally likely to be workaholics. The difference isn't in the prevalence; it's in the perception. My research shows that women may experience more negative outcomes than men from being overworkers. Women who put work first (even if they have stay-at-home partners) are still expected to handle the bulk of family responsibilities. Because of this, women workaholics often work more sporadic hours (late into the night, after putting the kids to bed), which in turn could fuel negative feelings about *not* working (since they are forced into other activities that feel like they're taking them away from what they want to do—work). In reality, women are just as likely as men to have workaholic tendencies—it just looks different.

suffered dearly because of their inability to respond to signals their bodies were giving them or to prioritize themselves over their work.

If they perceive they don't have enough to do, workaholics will look for more to add to their plate, taking on additional work projects and assignments above and beyond their normal job requirements, some of which they're neither qualified for nor positively contributing to. Take Lauren, for example. Lauren describes herself as a recovering workaholic and is a member of Workaholics Anonymous. When reflecting on her time in academia (a career she has since left), Lauren describes how she used to constantly volunteer to help with additional projects. When she didn't have an overwhelming workload or pressing deadline, she would get a knot in the pit of her stomach, a physical nausea that could be relieved only if she found pressing work to do. Ironically, this ended up being a self-fulfilling prophecy, because taking the extra work created situations where she actually *did* need to put in extra time to complete the additional job(s). For individuals like Lauren, working for the sake of working is the end goal, as opposed to a means to an end. And her inability to deal with her physical discomfort in any way except through adding work was a clear signal of workaholism.

Working more also means that work is brought into virtually every aspect of life—especially family and friends time, free time, and vacations. Workaholics often do this through a trick called "working lite," which involves incorporating activities associated with being off work to make it feel like they are not working, even though they are.[21] Working in front of the TV, or working poolside or on the beach, or having a glass of wine while working late into the night, or reading work-related materials for fun—these are all working lite strategies that are red flags. I'm guilty of this myself, often catching myself listening to work-related podcasts during my walks so I can continue to be "productive" during my non-work time or pulling out my laptop to respond to a few emails while I watch a TV show.

Notice again how little the number of hours worked matters in these scenarios. For Lauren, the hours she worked were a *result* of her workaholic tendencies, not a cause. She created the need for them. It's the excessive nature of and focus on work that is a signal.

Motivational: Inner Compulsion to Work

Another defining feature of workaholism is a constant feeling that you always need to be working, or you *ought to* be working. For me, it's a feeling in my gut, almost a feeling of restlessness and unease when I'm not *doing* something. For others, it might feel like a racing mind or a jittery unease.

The motivational core of workaholism is centered around the concept of introjected motivation discussed earlier in the chapter— partially internalized societal pressure to *never not work*. The work- aholic is someone who can never calm the inner voice that makes them feel like time not working is wasted time, or that they will be judged for not working—deemed less valuable or somehow a good candidate for being fired.

This inner pressure undoubtedly stems partially from internal- ized societal expectations about the ideal worker. But everyone feels those expectations, and not all individuals are workaholics, so there must be other factors at play too. Individual personality differences may come into it. For example, workaholism is highly related to hav- ing what's commonly referred to as a type A, do-it-all personality. Perfectionism is another personality trait highly related to work- aholism. Workaholics tend to feel that they don't live up to their own personal standards, that they are never good enough. Desea, a kindergarten teacher and member of Workaholics Anonymous,

Myth: Workaholism is innate and cannot be influenced by the environment

There is evidence that workaholism is something that starts quite early in life and seems to be related to personality traits such as type A personality and perfectionism. And certain people seem to have more workaholic tendencies than others. None of this is incorrect.

At the same time, there is a great deal of evidence that even what we had considered to be relatively stable "innate" characteristics, like our personalities, actually change across our lifetimes and become stronger or weaker depending on our external environments and specific situations. For example, many of you have probably heard of the Big Five personality traits (conscientiousness, agreeableness, extraversion, neuroticism, and openness), which are typically thought about as qualities that are stable over our life span. But even though someone has a general baseline level of these traits, researchers have shown that the levels do fluctuate and that these fluctuations are affected by our experiences. Management professor Timothy Judge, well known for his work on personality, demonstrated that Big Five personality traits fluctuate even from day to day, and that they are affected by our workplace experiences the prior day.[a] My colleagues and I extended this work to workaholism, finding that on mornings when people anticipated high workload, they experienced greater workaholic feelings, thoughts, and behaviors toward their work, which were in turn linked to greater fatigue that day as well as elevated systolic blood pressure.[b]

Does this mean that someone who does not hold any workaholic characteristics would become a workaholic if they were in the right job? Not likely. But if a person has some tendencies associated with obsessing over work, then when they're placed in an environment that encourages overworking, that environment can mold and shape them to bring out the workaholic within. Studies have shown, for example, that job demands are a predictor of future workaholism.[c] Additionally, having a high workload is a stronger predictor of workaholism than work engagement.[d]

a. Timothy A. Judge et al., "What I Experienced Yesterday Is Who I Am Today: Relationship of Work Motivations and Behaviors to Within-Individual Variation in the Five-Factor Model of Personality," *Journal of Applied Psychology* 99, no. 2 (2014): 199–221, https://doi.org/10.1037/a0034485.

b. Malissa A. Clark, Emily M. Hunter, and Dawn S. Calson, "Hidden Costs of Anticipated Workload for Individuals and Partners: Exploring the Role of Daily Fluctuations in Workaholism," *Journal of Occupational Health Psychology* 26, no. 5 (2021): 393–404, https://doi.org/10.1037/ocp0000284; Christian Balducci et al., "A Within-Individual Investigation on the Relationship between Day Level Workaholism and Systolic Blood Pressure," *Work and Stress* 36, no. 4 (2022): 337–354, https://doi.org/10.1080/02678373.2021.1976883.

c. Cristian Balducci, Lorenzo Avanzi, and Franco Fraccaroli, "The Individual 'Costs' of Workaholism: An Analysis Based on Multisource and Prospective Data," *Journal of Management* 44 (2018): 2961–2986, https://doi.org/10.1177/0149206316658348.

d. Nicolas Gillet et al., "Investigating the Combined Effects of Workaholism and Work Engagement: A Substantive-Methodological Synergy of Variable-Centered and Person-Centered Methodologies," *Journal of Vocational Behavior* 109 (2018): 54–77, https://doi.org/10.1016/j.jvb.2018.09.006.

remembers that her perfectionist tendencies manifested at a young age. She recalls how diligently she worked to make sure her class notes were as neat as possible and perfectly printed. Her room had to be super organized and tidy. Fast-forward to today, the same perfection applies to her kindergarten classroom. "The chairs all have to be pushed under the tables, each painting needs to be placed on the wall just so—spaced apart evenly, at the same height, every pencil sharpened, chalk and crayons organized by color, curtains have to be exactly symmetrical. I definitely have OCD about that." It's easy to see how these same inner desires for order, neatness, and completion can be applied to a work life in a way that starts to block out other parts of life.

Still, this compulsion or feeling of needing perfection doesn't necessarily have to be linked to work. It can extend to many other things—exercise, volunteering, various hobbies—and taking those activities to the extreme, too. The underlying compulsive nature of individuals is not restricted to the workplace, but societal expectations make work a prime place for these tendencies to manifest. As Debra, a private practitioner and member of Workaholics Anonymous, put it: "Workaholism is more than just about compulsive work. It's about compulsive activity and feeling compelled to always be doing." Others have labeled it an "addiction to busyness."

Cognitive: Constant Work Rumination

Workaholics think excessively about work. So many of the workaholics I've interviewed admit that work is the first thing that comes to their minds when they wake up and the last thing that they think about before they go to bed. Some have their sleep interrupted by thoughts of work. For example, Lauren described waking up at 3 a.m. thinking of an email she meant to send the day before or an upcoming project. To a non-workaholic, these may seem like small things that could wait until waking hours to address. It may seem surprising that something like an email would awaken you. Not for Lauren. Unable to go back to sleep, she would often begin working in the middle of the night and continue until her kids woke up and needed help getting ready for school. On her drive home from work at the end of the day, Lauren would record audio messages to herself on her phone for things she wanted to remind herself to do *when she got home*—that is, she was using her commute from work to ensure she could work when she got home from work. Then, before settling in to work, she would talk about work with her husband, and she would think about work while preparing dinner or spending time with her children. Reflecting now, Lauren says it was difficult to think of times when work was not front of mind.

The scholarly term for this behavior is *rumination*. Workaholics ruminate about their work all the time. This constant preoccupation that dominates one's mind is difficult, if not impossible, to shut off, especially when paired with the inner compulsion to work.

Constant work rumination is problematic for a variety of reasons. Most importantly, it prevents us from important recovery experiences. Anne-Marie, a retired social worker who has been a member of Workaholics Anonymous for decades, described to me how her workaholism prevented her from getting a good night's sleep because "it felt like my head was working all night long." Her doctor called this "non-restorative sleep," which left her feeling exhausted when she woke up because her head was processing all night long. Recovery experiences—not just getting restful sleep but also letting go of our work when we are awake—are essential processes that allow us to replenish the energy (mental and physical) that we expended during the workday.

Myth: Technology allows us to be more productive, thus reducing our workaholism

Your client wants to have a meeting with all its suppliers at the same time? Forget the hassle of hopping on a plane and traveling cross-country. This can be accomplished through a video call instead. Running a complicated statistical analysis? Analytics software can do it in mere seconds. This doesn't just apply to work tasks. Historian Ruth Schwartz Cowan describes the so-called time-saving capabilities of household devices such as washing machines and microwaves that shifted the work from servants and other hired help to the middle-class housewife in her book, *More Work for Mother.*[a] So, if technology has shaved off the time it used to take to accomplish various tasks, we should have more leisure time and all be working less, right? I think we all know the answer to this question. No.

So what gives? Historian C. Northcote Parkinson wrote in 1955 that "work expands so as to fill the time available for its completion."[b] It's now called Parkinson's Law. Although this idea can be applied in a variety of ways (for example, to explain why we procrastinate), in this instance,

Constant work rumination is detrimental for other reasons as well. It often means physical presence replaces *full* presence. Think of Lauren, who was there to help her kids get ready for school but whose mind was somewhere else. Others pick up on this mental and emotional distance, even if the workaholic thinks they're hiding it.

even though we have freed up time, we simply fill up that time with . . . more work. We don't work less because the analytics software works fast; we just *run millions more analyses on the data*.

Relatedly, in what has been coined the *autonomy paradox*, the more technology enables us to dictate where, when, and how we work, the more we end up working.[c] Workaholism is a growing problem *because* of technology. It allows ever-easier working lite—or working while doing non-work things as a way to trick yourself into thinking you're not working (checking Slack conversations after dinner, bringing work on vacation, waking up early to get a head start on the overnight email). The double-edged sword of technology is real. It seamlessly smudges into the rest of our lives, creating a ripe environment for breeding workaholics.

a. Ruth Schwartz Cowan, *More Work for Mother: The Ironies of Household Technology from the Open Hearth to the Microwave* (New York: Basic Books, 1983).

b. C. Northcote Parkinson, "Parkinson's Law," *Economist*, November 19, 1955, https://www.economist.com/news/1955/11/19 /parkinsons-law.

c. Melissa Mazmanian, Wanda J. Orlikowski, and JoAnne Yates, "The Autonomy Paradox: The Implications of Mobile Email Devices for Knowledge Professionals," *Organization Science* 24, no. 5 (2013): 1337–1357, https://doi.org/10.1287/orsc.1120.0806.

Indeed, "inability to disconnect" and "often distracted" were commonly mentioned in my interviews of spouses of workaholics. One person even noted that they were seeing increased conflict among their children, who were battling to win their workaholic parent's limited attention.

Emotional: Negative Feelings When Not Working

When they are not working, workaholics are often plagued by anxiety and guilt. If circumstances or individuals prevent them from working, they experience frustration, irritation, and anger.

The anxiety is driven by many factors, including imaginary narratives they've created. In the mind of a workaholic, not working may mean people are judging them for slacking off. It may mean they think they will be exposed as a fraud. It may mean they will never get a promotion. These are powerful stories the mind tells a person that are designed to make them feel bad, because the antidote to feeling bad is to work.

Desea, the kindergarten teacher who discussed her perfectionist tendencies, also talked about her fear of not having enough time as a driving factor behind her incessant need to work all the time. Everything had an urgency to it and needed to be done right away. "I can't waste a minute during my vacation. I have to plan all my vacation right now because I can't waste any time."

Guilt stems from always feeling there is more that needs to be done. Think about your to-do list for the day or week. If it's anything like mine, it seems never-ending. As things get checked off, additional tasks are added, resulting in a list that is never fully completed. For the workaholic, this unfinished to-do list can plant constant stress in the body, leading the workaholic to continue plugging away. Part of this is likely related to the workaholic's perfectionism—it's difficult to let something go if it is not fully completed.

For many workaholics, there is no legitimate excuse for *not* working, so any activity that detracts from working is likely to make the workaholic feel guilty. Workaholics I've interviewed have mentioned feeling guilty about taking time off work to attend important life events such as a family reunion, weddings, even funerals.

I can, unfortunately, relate to this. I gave birth to both of my kids when I was in graduate school, and at that time there was no parental leave for graduate students at my university (thankfully, it's better now). My daughter Alex was born in the middle of the semester—not ideal, since at that time I was taking a class and teaching a section on workplace psychology. Rather than brainstorming alternative ways to finish the semester, in my workaholic brain, the only possible option was to prove that I was a "good graduate student" by taking as little time off as possible (taking only a week off from my class and teaching after Alex's birth). As ridiculous as it sounds, I felt guilty for inconveniencing others and didn't want to put anyone out by asking for help. I also didn't want to be perceived as not committed to my graduate studies, even though I know my adviser would have supported me taking more time. So, as the due date got closer, I frantically worked absurd hours and pulled in as much work as I could. The afternoon before Alex was born, I worked on my midterm while timing my contractions, trying to utilize every last minute before *actually giving birth* forced me to take an unwanted break.

Notice how I, the workaholic, could easily think about the ways I was letting work down by deigning to give birth, but I couldn't as easily see how I might be letting other people in my life down—including my child!—by putting work above all. This is the pernicious way workaholism starts to crowd out everything but work, making it hard for the person to see even easy contradictions in their thinking and in the narratives they've created in their heads.

Workaholics will begin to see outside presences in their lives—children, spouses, friends, and family—as barriers to work. As opposed to feeling as though their work encroaches on their family time, workaholics feel the opposite—that family demands encroach on their ability to work.

. . .

This is likely the most nuanced view of workaholism you've read. It's important that we dig into the details and have a complete picture of what marks workaholism and what does and does not contribute to its proliferation if we're to prevent it in ourselves and others.

I've noted already how the words *workaholism* and *workaholic* are not ideal. One of the problems I've encountered with them is the louche way they are treated, used as casual badges of a certain personality for people who don't exhibit the real traits of workaholics. This casual deployment—similar to how people might proudly say "Oh, I'm a total shopaholic" or coyly confess, "I'm definitely a massive chocoholic"—belies something more serious. You have started to see, and will come to see more fully in the coming pages, that true workaholism is a serious detriment to individuals and organizations. So, let's get to spotting it, addressing it, and fixing it.

Workaholism Self-Assessment

You may have read this chapter and thought to yourself that some of the attributes I've noted resonated with you. Or you may have thought, *This really applies to someone I know.* If you are in charge of people in an organization in some capacity, you may wonder if there's a way to find out who among you is displaying workaholic behavior.

Good news: I've created an assessment to find out. Here is a basic version of that assessment (a full version is found in the appendix, and I've also included the Workaholics Anonymous assessment there).

Read the statements and rate the degree to which each item describes you using the following scale:

---

1 = never true   2 = seldom true   3 = sometimes true
4 = often true   5 = always true

---

1. I work because there is a part inside of me that feels compelled to work. _____

2. It is difficult for me to stop thinking about work when I stop working. _____

3. I feel upset if I have to miss a day of work for any reason. _____

4. I tend to work beyond my job's requirements. _____

Now, add up your total score across the four items. Your score will range between 1 and 20.

A good rule of thumb is that if your total score is 15 or above, you are displaying significant signs of workaholism. Even if you score below that, if you scored 4 or 5 on any of these items, you have some workaholic tendencies.

Key Takeaways

- Workaholism is on the rise and is detrimental for the workaholics, those around them, and their organizations.

- Workaholism is more than just working long hours; it involves four key components: behavioral, motivational, cognitive, and emotional.

- Workaholism is not a clinical condition.

- Workaholism lies on a spectrum; even those with a few workaholic tendencies may be at risk for negative consequences.

- There is no "good" workaholism.

- Workaholics are not more productive.

- Men and women are equally likely to be workaholics.

- Technology has exacerbated our workaholic tendencies.

CHAPTER 2

A Portrait of the Modern Workaholic

> When work becomes more important than anything else, you develop a pattern of forgetting, ignoring, or minimizing the importance of family rituals and celebrations. You miss your child's final bow. You forget the birthday party. And even if you do make it to an event, you might have trouble concentrating because your mind is back at the office.
>
> —Psychotherapist Bryan E. Robinson, in *#Chill*

"It's cancer."

Ellen, a retired education leader, recalls this harrowing moment in her life. Her mammogram had revealed a lump in her breast. Devastating news for anyone. But Ellen was more worried about the effect on her work. She recalls, "Here the doctor is telling me I need to have a lumpectomy and I'm negotiating. I need to do it right before my scheduled vacation in a month so that there would be fewer days I'd need to take off work for my recovery."

What Ellen didn't know was how aggressive her adversary was. "And guess what? It turns out, it was a very fast-growing cancer, and it had doubled in size between then and my vacation. I had put myself at life-and-death risk—but for what?"

Ellen's story is not unique; I've spoken with many workaholics who tell similar stories of deprioritizing their own well-being. For a workaholic, the most important consideration at a critical life moment—a life-threatening moment—may still be their work. Work is prioritized above all else, to their own detriment and to the detriment of their loved ones. Of course, at a less critical level, that also means it's a detriment to organizations, which shouldn't want to be the source of someone's poor health.

Ellen survived, but other workaholics may not be so lucky. The workplace ranks as the fifth leading cause of death in America. Studies have found that long work hours increase mortality by almost 20 percent.[1] Recall the Japanese term *karoshi*—"work until you die." Brigid Schulte, author of *Overwhelmed: How to Work, Love, and Play When No One Has the Time*, has devoted an entire season of her podcast *Better Life Lab* to the perils of what she calls "American karoshi."[2]

To show just how insidious a threat to health workaholism is, we'll hear more stories like Ellen's, buttressed by data. Read on to understand the real physical effects of workaholism, but also to see if you recognize any of these behaviors or symptoms in yourself or someone you know.

Signs of Workaholic Behavior

If you're concerned you or someone else might fall prey to workaholism, there are signs of what to look out for. Note that we all exhibit some of these behaviors sometimes—who hasn't wanted to get something at work perfect and put in extra time to get there? The difference here is the "always" of it. Workaholics display these behaviors constantly. Let's look at four of these "always behaviors": rumination, overcommitment, busyness, and perfectionism.

Rumination: Always Thinking about Work

Workaholics obsess about work constantly. This preoccupation is difficult, if not impossible, for them to shut off. And when others try to focus on something other than work, the workaholic will be uncomfortable, irritated, or even angry.

Overcommitment: Always Taking On Too Much and Not Knowing Limits

A key element to compulsive work is the drive to add work into life at every opportunity. Take Albert, who described how working sixty hours a week gave him adequate room for . . . more work. "There was a lot more time to do other things," he said. "So I started another business."[3] Veronica, a psychotherapist in private practice, spoke about how sneaky and seductive workaholism was—like the sirens tempting Odysseus with their beautiful and enchanting, but deadly, songs. In her case, through her dedication to recovery in Workaholics Anonymous, Veronica was able to successfully manage her workaholism when came to her paid job, only to find herself clocking in twelve-hour days between her job and a passion project of hers—writing for a documentary series. Thankfully, she said, the series wasn't picked up. But through that experience, she learned she could just as easily fall back into her workaholic habits around creative endeavors.

Workaholics do not know or ignore their physical limits. Many times, they will plow on until their bodies physically give up. Take Desea, the kindergarten teacher we met in chapter 1. Her workaholism was so severe at one point she had to take nineteen weeks' leave; she said her body just gave out on her one day, as if it had said, "You know what? If you're not going to take a break, I'm going to take a break and make you listen."

When your mind tells you to fill every available minute with work, it feels devastating when work is not possible, and this can lead to depressive symptoms and emotional distress. After being diagnosed with health issues severe enough to prevent her from working, Sarah, a nonprofit entrepreneur who has been a member of Workaholics Anonymous for the past five years, wasn't thinking about improving her health. Instead, she was asking herself questions like, "Why am I even still living? What purpose do I have?"

When your identity is so intertwined with work, and you don't know or don't respect limits, removing work creates existential crises. Several of my interviewees discussed severe bouts of depression and suicidal ideation or attempts. The worst part is the workaholic may see it coming and still not be able to stop. Chris, an IT professional, has struggled with his workaholism for more than thirty years. He knew he was hitting his breaking point—said it felt like a train crash waiting to happen, as he was both physically and mentally exhausted—but he kept telling himself he could work through it, because he had done so in the past. He rationalized his workaholism to himself, saying, "I have to work late into the evening because of the time zone" (he is in Europe and often deals with US clients); "It'll be a catastrophe if I don't finish this project"; or "I don't want to make my coworker work during the holiday, so I'll do it myself." Chris's typical day was waking up at 6 a.m., working by 7:30, and working ten- to twelve-hour days. He would come home, eat dinner, have his tea, go for a walk, and continue working until about midnight. Eventually, he found himself working this schedule seven days a week. He'd go to bed exhausted but unable to sleep because he would stay up all night worrying.

But there was a breaking point. After doing this for years, he found himself in tears before he went into work. Problems at work kept getting bigger and bigger. Finally, giving in to his wife's pleas to go to the doctor, he was diagnosed with severe anxiety and depression. He was prescribed medication, but he refused to take it and kept trying to power through at work. It wasn't working, and a week after the doctor visit, he tried to take his own life.

In his mind, Chris had had enough. Today, he says he is in a much better place. Someone else took on his old role in the company. He takes great effort to manage his workaholic urges and to prioritize self-care. He admits to having an addictive personality, so he must constantly remind himself not to give in to the urge to work more. He also has created some unique strategies to help calm his workaholic thoughts, one of which is to create what he calls a "memory box." He told me, "When I'm ready to stop working that day, I physically put my phone away in a box. This prevents me from constantly checking my email. It was really the only way I could truly disconnect, because otherwise, the temptation was just too strong."

Busyness: Always Doing

Even if someone isn't taking on too much, they could be showing workaholic tendencies if they are always doing some work. This manifests as constant busyness. Work may not be overwhelming, but it's always present. This is driven biologically by a need for the adrenaline we experience when we are feeling stressed, which is often itself driven by a fear we aren't doing enough.

Lauren described this as a sense that she needed to be contributing to her work all the time. Like many workaholics, she would check her email constantly throughout the evening or on weekends. She would read online articles when she was relaxing in front of the TV or listen to work-related podcasts when exercising. She would read articles and highlight things that she wanted to incorporate into her research while running on the treadmill. Laughing, she added, "Do you know how hard it is to run and highlight at the same time?"

To the workaholic, even play is work. Hobbies become obsessions. Adult coloring books are touted as a tool to relax and decompress. But recovering workaholic Sarah recalls her tendency to turn adult coloring books into a kind of work project. "I gotta finish this page," she would tell herself. "My hand will be cramping. There's no good reason I need to finish this page of coloring." But she couldn't seem to stop. And then there's retired social worker Anne-Marie, who recounts how she ignored her needs even when it came to her gardening hobby. "I'd go out to the garden for hours on end," she told me, "so engrossed in my gardening that I'd forget to eat, drink, or use the toilet. I'd regularly work until I was so exhausted that I couldn't put away my tools or even cook dinner—I'd just collapse in my bed and pass out from sheer exhaustion."

Of course, workaholics turn vacations into work, too. We've also seen how the time *around* vacations becomes especially important to workaholics, who become consumed with the idea that they *have to* work harder before and after to make up for the time off (which won't be time off). This of course affects the people around them, especially family members who want to relax on vacation. Chris, for example, talked about how when he had a vacation, he would work late into the night before they left for their holiday. He would have his wife drive to and from the airport so he could work in the back of the car.

What you will notice with workaholics is not just that they're always doing, but that there is always *structure* to what they're doing. Unstructured time feels uncomfortable for a workaholic. They cannot cope with feeling not only like they're not doing anything but also that the time is being wasted because there's no plan for how to use it.

All this always doing is often worn as a badge of honor to signal their importance and value—to others and to themselves. That's in part because busyness is rewarded in modern culture, because it looks like productivity. In fact, they're not the same. Think about your own organization. Do you actively or passively reward busyness? Do you shout out to the colleague who put in the extra time on the weekend? Do you talk about the number of hours someone put in on a project as a positive? You may be encouraging workaholic behaviors. The culture of busyness is a pervasive one, but we will see later there are ways to combat it.

Perfectionism: Nothing Is Ever Good Enough

It's natural to want to do our best, but for perfectionists, "our best" is simply not good enough. In my research I've linked each of the components of workaholism to perfectionism, which involves being overly critical of one's own performance and setting excessively high standards.[4] This research doesn't tell us whether perfectionism drives workaholism or vice versa, just that they are strongly related. However, given the majority of workaholics I have interviewed who cite their perfectionist tendencies as one of the factors that contributed to their workaholism (and reflecting on my own workaholic tendencies, I definitely agree), I'd say it's likely the former.

Gender and workaholism

The research on the effects of workaholism for different genders is nascent but starting to provide some insight on the differing effects for men and women. And as with many gender dynamics, this one doesn't seem to favor women.

Men can fall back on the breadwinner trope as a reason to obsess about work. This doesn't make their workaholism less of a problem, but it might mean that the physical and mental toll isn't as severe as it is for women, who must face the additional societal and internalized scrutiny of being expected to be the "ideal mother" in addition to being always on at work. It's a recipe for overextension for someone with workaholic behaviors. Take Lauren, for example, who confessed that she put a lot of pressure on herself to be the ideal worker since she felt like she wasn't living up to her role as the prototypical ideal mother. She admits she felt some judgment about her decision to work full-time in a demanding career and some subtle pressure from her circle, including other moms in her neighborhood to make it "worth it." These offhand comments implied "I hope your career is worth leaving your kids to be raised

What Drives Adverse Health Effects in Workaholics?

The above stories will start to give you a sense of the real and sometimes harrowing effects of workaholism on the person who can't disconnect from work. But these aren't mere anecdotes or isolated cases; they are part of a pattern of outcomes that are predictable based by someone else," exacerbating the pressure she put on herself to be the best that she possibly could be at her job. "I felt like, if you're going to put all of this time and effort into a career, you'd better make it count. You can't just do a good job. If you're going to be making all these sacrifices, you'd better shine."

A study on daily workaholism and blood pressure found that the relationship between workaholism and high blood pressure was stronger for women.[a] My meta-analysis showed a stronger link between workaholism and negative health outcomes for women than for men. In fact, I found that the relationship between workaholism and health issues was stronger as the percentage of women in the sample increased.[b]

More research is needed, but early evidence from studies and my anecdotal evidence from talking to both women and men who are or were workaholics, I can see that interventions may need to be tailored to the different experiences of different genders.

a. Cristian Balducci et al., "A Within-Individual Investigation on the Relationship between Day Level Workaholism and Systolic Blood Pressure," *Work and Stress* 36, no. 4 (2022): 337–354, doi: 10.1080/02678373.2021.1976883.

b. Malissa A. Clark, Rachel Williamson Smith, and Nicholas J. Haynes, "The Multidimensional Workaholism Scale: Linking the Conceptualization and Measurement of Workaholism," *Journal of Applied Psychology* 105, no. 11 (2020): 1281–1307, https://doi.org/10.1037/apl0000484.

on the data. My colleagues and I compiled findings across dozens of published articles and found a significant relationship between workaholism and poor health.[5] (And within that finding, there's also a significant relationship between the way workaholism affects the health of men versus women; see "Gender and workaholism.")

Before I dive into specifics of these poor health effects, let's take a big-picture view of the two key physical drivers of these poor health outcomes: workaholics' constant fight-or-flight mode, and their lack of effective recovery experiences.

Workaholics Operate in Constant Fight-or-Flight Mode

When we are faced with stress or a threat, we are hardwired to automatically go into fight-or-flight mode, where our bodies prepare to fight against an imminent threat.[6] When this happens, we have a physiological reaction as our autonomic nervous system is activated—increased heart rate and rapid breathing, for example. Our body also increases its production of the stress hormone cortisol, which stimulates the liver to release an increased supply of glucose directly to our muscles (to give us strength) and diverts it away from other organ systems that are not as important in the moment—such as the digestive system and immune system. Again, in a crisis, this efficiency can be extremely beneficial. Finally, to deal with an immediate threat, our hypothalamus activates our sympathetic nervous system to release epinephrine (adrenaline). This adrenaline surge and increased supply of glucose has been known to give us seemingly superhero strength in a crisis. I'm reminded of a story of Tom Boyle Jr., who miraculously was able to lift a three-thousand-pound car off a cyclist who was pinned underneath it, and thus save his life.[7]

Although this response is advantageous in emergency situations, when our bodies are constantly in fight-or-flight mode, it can cause many problems. For example, excess cortisol has been linked to the development of hypertension and a sustained accelerated heart rate, which can lead to elevated resting blood pressure. Scientists have explained the detrimental effects of sustained fight-or-flight mode primarily through the concept of *allostasis*—our body's way of maintaining homeostasis (stability) by temporarily changing and adapting to environmental demands. According to the allostatic load model, the stress process first involves a period of initial adaptation through the activation process.[8] In a healthy coping response, after the threat goes away, the body calms itself and goes back to homeostasis. However, if these systems are chronically activated, as they are for a workaholic, over time this constant stimulation affects our bodies in the same way that a two-thousand-mile road trip can cause wear and tear on a car. When these systems are consistently dysregulated (out of normal range), they serve as key risk factors for a variety of negative long-term physical and mental outcomes, including cardiovascular disease, chronic illnesses, diabetes, clinical depression, and in extreme cases, even death.[9]

Workaholics Suffer from a Lack of Effective Recovery Experiences

The second reason workaholism negatively affects our health has to do with how our bodies recover from stress. There is a cumulative effect of strain on our bodies, so as we work more, we need even more recovery.

This is why there are diminishing returns on excess time spent working. Economist John Pencaval has been studying this phenomenon for decades. He argues that we need to make a distinction between nominal hours of work (the number of hours someone spends at work) and effective hours of work (the number of hours we are *effective* while working). Based on the idea of diminishing returns, we will gain fewer effective hours of work as we add to our nominal hours. At a certain point, we start to lose effective hours.[10] For example, imagine two workers, Susan and Larry. Susan has already put in thirty hours of work for the week and Larry has already put in forty. One more hour of work will be a much more productive hour for Susan than it will be for Larry, because Larry's body is already more fatigued from the time he has spent working. In fact, after about fifty-five hours of work, for every nominal hour of work, the number of effective hours of work decreases (picture an upside down U). Pencavel's model shows that someone who works seventy hours is no more productive than someone who puts in fifty-five hours.

What Are the Specific Health Effects of Workaholism?

With these two broad drivers of poor health outcomes, we can dive into the specific things that research shows are linked to workaholism.

Heart Disease

Working long hours is detrimental to heart health. For example, 10 to 20 percent of all cardiovascular disease deaths among the working-age populations can be attributed to work.[11] Three to four hours of overtime work per day is associated with a 60 percent increased risk of incident coronary heart disease compared with employees who do not work overtime.[12] In a study that followed American workers over a twenty-five-year period, researchers found that individuals working seventy-five hours or more per week were *twice* as likely to experience cardiovascular disease than individuals working forty-five hours per week.[13] Long work hours also have been linked to other cardiovascular risk factors such as high blood pressure and increased risk of stroke.[14]

But remember, long hours alone don't make a workaholic. How much of these negative effects are driven by workaholism, specifically? Well, there is convincing data directly linking workaholism and cardiovascular risk factors. In one study, researchers conducted physical exams for more than 750 Dutch workers at a financial consulting firm. No relationship was found between work hours and risk factors of metabolic syndrome. Workaholism, however, was positively related to increased risk. Thus, it was an employee's compulsive work mentality—not just the fact that they worked long hours—that was driving the increased cardiovascular risk.[15] Another study led by Dr. Marisa Salanova studied more than five hundred employees in several different hospitals in Spain. Most were nurses and laboratory technicians. Workaholics showed the strongest relationship with cardiovascular risk compared with other workers, and they had the highest probability of suffering a cardiovascular event in the next ten years.[16]

Building on this work, my colleagues and I wanted to further examine whether workaholism was related to cardiovascular risk factors on a day-to-day basis. Each evening for two weeks, we asked workers to record their level of workaholic thoughts (how much they continued to think about work after finishing for the day) and workaholic feelings (feeling like they ought to be continuously working that day), and we had them assess their resting systolic blood pressure using a device we provided. On evenings they reported thinking about and doing work after hours, we found that they had increased blood pressure.[17]

Weakened Autoimmune Responses

There is also evidence of a link between workaholism and immune system function. A feature of our immune system—a protein called a *cytokine*—plays a critical (yet complicated) role in regulating our body's immune system functioning. Say, for example, you cut your hand. Your body sends reinforcements to the point of injury to deal with the emergency threat. Cytokines that would ordinarily serve various functions throughout your body are diverted directly to your injured hand as part of this immune response. Your immune cells work hard to patch up the damaged tissue by "recruiting" other immune cells and diverting them from their normal duties to form a scab. Eventually, the scab falls off once the immune cells have sufficiently rebuilt the damaged tissues and broken blood vessels. In this way, cytokines can serve a protective function, shielding your body from pathogens and other diseases by signaling that an immune response is necessary.[18]

However, it is not just cuts or other physical injuries that can trigger an immune response. Any sort of environmental threat (real or perceived) can also trigger this immune response. And if the threat persists or never resolves itself, our bodies remain in a state of chronic inflammation, fighting an imaginary cut that has long since healed. Chronic inflammation reflects chronic dysregulation of our immune systems, which contributes to any number of inflammatory and autoimmune diseases such as psoriasis, rheumatoid arthritis, asthma, lupus, and even cancerous tumor development and progression.[19]

Recent findings linking workaholism to activating specific cytokines highlight the potential widespread implications of workaholism in a variety of diseases linked to our body's immune response. Researchers in Italy examined the relationship between workaholism and one particular cytokine called interleukin-17.[20] Controlling for other relevant factors such as gender, age, and body mass index, the research team found that workaholism was related to higher levels of interleukin-17, evidence of heightened inflammation.

These research findings are in line with the types of physical ailments workaholics have described to me. Take Annelyse, a real estate professional and member of Workaholics Anonymous. Looking back, Annelyse attributes her ongoing health issues primarily to her extreme workaholism. For many years, she battled a series of physical conditions including shingles, weekly vertigo spells, heart palpitations, and extreme fatigue. One time, when her workaholism was at its worst, Annelyse remembers fainting when she was simultaneously dealing with her five-year-old daughter's meltdown and a failing real estate deal. After regaining consciousness, Annelyse found she couldn't talk or move. After numerous tests at the hospital, doctors diagnosed her with dehydration and exhaustion. She received strict doctor's orders to slow down (which, of course, she didn't). Only after many years in Workaholics Anonymous does Annelyse recognize she was suffering from extreme burnout resulting from her inability to detach from work. Based on what we know now about the relationship between workaholism and immune-related diseases, many of Annelyse's mysterious symptoms may have been directly or indirectly linked to her extreme devotion to work. When she was at the mercy of her workaholism, it felt to Annelyse that she was dealing with one health ailment after another. For example, for years she was plagued by a rash that doctors could only identify as eczema. Despite treatment and medication, it continued to worsen; it got so bad that her hands were covered in boils. Of course, like many health issues, it could not be directly linked to a single cause. Our bodies are complex systems. Still, Annelyse is quick to point out that many of her health issues have resolved themselves since she has gotten her workaholism under control.

Then there's Sarah, introduced earlier in this chapter, whose illnesses started with pneumonia, which spurred a host of chronic symptoms, including extreme fatigue, that eventually prevented her from working. After a year of tests and unanswered questions, Sarah made her way to a Mayo Clinic, where she was diagnosed with a very rare form of vasculitis. Sarah is currently on disability, as she is physically unable to work more than three hours per week.

But Sarah's identity and entire way of being revolved around work. While you may feel relief at getting a diagnosis and resting to recover, Sarah described the point when she was forced to acknowledge that she could no longer work full-time as "heartbreaking." Her vasculitis likely had complex causes, but Sarah admits that her workaholic tendencies "sure as hell did not help it."

And then there's Gabe, who has battled a series of serious and rare chronic illnesses since the age of twenty-five. Like Sarah, Gabe's health issues became so severe at one point that he was physically unable to work. He recalls going through feelings of extreme withdrawal when his health issues prevented him from working at all and he was forced to take several weeks off: "Once the busyness left, I just crashed."

Many workaholics I've interviewed simply did not take the time to properly care for their bodies. I remember talking with Rebecca, a mother of two children who was married to a workaholic. She was desperately venting about how her husband prioritized work to the detriment of his own health—neglecting exercise and even routine dentist and doctor visits:

> My husband hasn't been to the doctor in so long that they insisted they had to treat him as a new patient. I finally put my foot down earlier this year and told him, "Honey, you're almost fifty-four and you haven't had a routine checkup in umpteen years. You need to have a checkup." Forget asking him when is good for him—he will just brush me off and say he needs to look at his schedule. So, sometimes I have to be the bad guy and just take it upon myself to schedule his checkups at the doctor and dentist. But I find it quite

ridiculous that I have to do these things. He's a grown man. I am his wife, after all—not his mother.

Then there's Ivy, who is now retired but has worked in a variety of different occupations, including lab technician, adjunct professor, and even llama ranch manager. Ivy recalls how she would set herself goals for all the work she had to do before she'd allow herself to eat or use the bathroom. "I'd tell myself that I have to package and ship every single order that came in before I could pee. So, I would be very hungry and running on adrenaline and needing to pee. But I just had to get that stuff done, or I would feel like I was no good."

Poor Sleep

Workaholics report a variety of sleep issues, including poor sleep quality, trouble falling asleep, not sleeping enough hours, feeling tired in the morning, and falling asleep when they're not supposed to (including falling asleep while driving).[21] Even when they do sleep, that slumber is often non-restorative due to the constant work rumination. Recall Anne-Marie, who said that even while she slept, "it felt like my head was working all night long." Others echo her feelings, reporting an inability to sleep even though they were physically exhausted.

We all know how important sleep is for our health. Thus, it is not surprising that poor sleep has been identified as one of the linking mechanisms between workaholism and cardiovascular risk.[22]

Anxiety and Depression

The negative self-appraisals that come from always needing to be perfect and failing to live up to impossibly high standards often manifest as anxiety and depression. Indeed, workaholics are more likely to report depressive symptoms and may be as much as 2.5 times more likely to experience a major depressive episode than the average worker.[23]

Other Addictions

One way that workaholics attempt to quell their feelings of having to be connected to work is to seek some relief through self-medicating or developing alternative addictions. For Lauren, workaholism fueled alcoholism. In fact, she came to learn about the concept of workaholism through her road to recovery from her alcoholism. Surprisingly, she is a former assistant professor specializing in substance abuse and addiction treatment. Her knowledge and her own struggle helped her see how similar aspects of her two addictions were. She now works full-time as a consultant, coach, and trainer and has conducted workshops on work addiction to many organizations, including the Secret Service.

Lauren and other addiction therapists have likened workaholism to other addictions such as alcoholism.[24] In both cases, you are outsourcing or delegating management of your emotional processes to something else. It may work temporarily, but then it backfires. Lauren describes workaholism as a type of process addiction—not just addiction to work (although that's part of it), but more than that, it's feeling addicted to the adrenaline, the physiological hormonal response, that comes from working: "The racing and the busyness and the addiction to achievements and accolades and awards and grants and publications and titles. But then it's overlapping in the sense that it's an addiction to the process, that pressure, and that productivity."

Lauren further goes on to explain how for her, workaholism and alcohol addiction had their own symbiotic relationship:

I think one of the metaphors I used, and I guess what it was like was the perfect speedball, where the work, the adrenaline was the go, go, go, achieve, achieve, achieve, win, win, win, and be recognized. But that's the stimulant, the cocaine, in the speedball. And that's what revs you up. That's what gets you high. And then there's the downer or the depressant—the alcohol—that calms you down. I needed that alcohol to calm back down. And so that's the opioid in the speedball. And you ideally kind of strike that tenuous balance between the two opposing effects.

Lauren recalls how she began to progressively increase her reliance on alcohol through her progression through graduate school and early in her career. It was only two years into her sobriety from alcohol use disorder that she began to fully realize the interrelatedness of her workaholism and alcohol addiction. When asked how she came to realize that the "primary" addiction was her workaholism, Lauren pinpoints the realization that managing her alcohol addiction and leaving academia did not solve her work patterns and identity struggles.

. . .

The pernicious effect of all these maladies that are woven into workaholism is how they lead to any number of second- and third-order effects that spill back into work. Exhausted workers are less creative, less patient with others, more prone to mistakes. Workers with chronic conditions miss more work.

This can set up a vicious cycle. If someone is always doing but suddenly they can't do, they get even more upset. If someone is always seeking perfection but starts to make mistakes because they're not sleeping, it further reinforces their obsessive ruminating about work.

In fact, all the health issues that are associated with or exacerbated by workaholic behavior are bad for organizations. Notice how, in the above stories, the workers ended up in the exact situation they thought they could engineer out of their lives: being out of work, sometimes for extended periods, which felt like a kind of death to them. That's bad for the person and for the company.

It's unlikely that workaholism is the sole cause of all these poor outcomes for people and their businesses, but it's clear it's deeply part of the equation, and possibly one that's more capable of being dealt with than others. While I can't do much to change my genetic predisposition to certain medical conditions, if my addiction to work is making it an untenable part of my life, I can work on that. If there is a chance that workaholism is going to increase my chances of developing cancer, well, then, I'm going to do my best to decrease those odds, particularly because cancer runs in my family. If my organization actively encourages or passively allows a culture that activates workaholic behavior and doesn't try to spot its workaholics and help them before it's too late, then I'm fostering a less productive, less healthy workforce.

Fortunately, there are ways to spot signs of workaholic behavior in yourself and others.

Effects of Workaholism on Those around the Workaholic

It's not just the workaholics who suffer these negative effects. Those around the workaholic also suffer collateral damage. These negative effects have been well documented in the clinical psychology area by scholars such as Bryan Robinson, among others.[25]

At Home

Sometimes the most powerful examples of the negative effects of workaholism come from workaholics' loved ones. In my research lab, we have interviewed more than fifty spouses of workaholics to gain an understanding of how workaholism affects families. Comparing these responses to the responses we received from the workaholics themselves makes it clear that workaholics underestimate the detrimental effects of their workaholism on their loved ones.

Chris realized the deep impact his workaholism had on his family by watching his son's approach to work. His son, now in his twenties, has told him that he intends to take a completely different attitude toward work because he has seen Chris working all the time. "I'm not going to be like you," he told Chris. He was going to enjoy his weekends and travel, using work to pay for his lifestyle, but that it would not be his life. Chris's workaholism also took a toll on his marriage. While some marriages struggle through infidelity, Chris says, "She didn't have to deal with me having a mistress because work was the mistress." Once, he left a seven-day vacation with his wife after day two to attend a conference.

Another spouse of a workaholic said something similar: "I know he's never having an affair. He's always at work [laugh]. I don't know. I feel like if anything, we mostly fight about me wanting him to spend more time with us." Interestingly, she then went on to try to rationalize what she clearly saw as troublesome behavior: "So, I guess if we have to fight about something, it's not a bad thing to be our main fight. You're busy—you don't get into trouble in that sense." This is common as people try to support the person by looking for ways to explain the behavior away or make it more palatable.

Here are a few more snippets of what the loved ones of workaholics said when asked about how it affected their marriages and families. I've left them mostly unedited so you can sense the kind of frustration and grasping for answers they seem to be going through:

> It has definitely affected our romantic relationship. Because you get angry. You're angry, so if you're angry, you don't want to be with someone intimately. Like it's a catch-22, you do and you don't. You're so pissed off because they're not here and the work has consumed them so much, but that then when you are together, it creates arguments because then he's bringing up work still, so there is no silence. There is no silence for there to be any real intimacy or relationship because it's created so many other issues.

> I feel like the kids are being cheated out of their father. And I'm ultimately being cheated out of my husband.

> [His workaholism] leaves me alone with our two children most of the time. I'm the one who is in charge of all the emotional workload, and all the workload, and it's stressful and at times overwhelming.

> I can't tell you the amount of times that I've eaten dinner alone. . . . Having to sleep alone sometimes affects me. Knowing that I have a child on the way and there's probably going to be days and nights where I don't even see him is worrisome, and of course, it affects me.

> I have canceled two appointments to file for divorce. And we are heading to an intensive couples therapy in a few weeks as a last-ditch attempt to save this.

We have a five-year-old and almost one-year-old. . . . They're used to a life without their dad.

My kids don't really have a relationship with their dad. I hate to say that that way, but he's not really been around pretty much for years. . . . Like they'll talk to him like you would talk to anybody else on the street. They don't have parent-child conversations.

She doesn't see the kids a lot. My son is five, and he recently said, "All dads do everything for all families," which made me realize that he definitely notices that she's not around.

He leaves on a Monday around 4 a.m. and comes back on Friday. Sometimes the kids won't even notice he was gone for five days. It's hard to describe, but it's almost like he is invisible to them now. They simply just don't depend on him a lot. They will walk past him to ask me for things.

It's so sad. You know, they'll even say to me, "Gosh, Mom, it's like we only have one parent." It hurts your soul. They're so used to him being gone that when he does come to their game or school event, they're shocked. They think something's wrong.

Notice in these quotes how workaholism doesn't just affect the amount of time spent with family and loved ones, but it also affects the *quality* of interactions even when the workaholic is present, because they are still working in their heads. This also frequently results in others feeling sad or lonely.

At Work

The negative impact of workaholic behavior also affects others around the workaholic in the workplace. In chapter 1, I discussed the research findings showing that workaholism did not result in increased productivity or performance; in fact, it can leave workers more burned-out and less engaged because they are not taking the time to recover from the time and energy they devote to their work. Adding to that, workaholism can also affect the performance of those who rely on or work with the workaholic. As desperate as some of the family members' pleas above feel, these are people who ostensibly love or want to love the person who can't detach themselves from work. Colleagues are less invested in the person but in some ways just as reliant on them. So when workaholism starts to affect relationships at work, it can be frustrating or even toxic to a team.

There are ways to spot typical indicators of potentially toxic workaholic behavior in your organization. Some of these behaviors could be signs of a burgeoning problem.

Letting perfect be the enemy of good. Perfectionist tendencies lead workaholics to spend too much time on tasks, which in turn affects others' ability to do their jobs. Say Jamal needs to write part of a presentation for a team briefing. He spends three full workdays getting his five slides just right, preventing others from working on their portions of the presentation. What's more, when he sees what others have done, he wants to redo their parts to match up with his in a way he finds acceptable. This is no problem for Jamal, who will constantly think about ways to make the presentation better and work extra hours to do it. But it hampers his teammates' efforts and it's overkill for the context. The presentation could have been good enough with a third of the work put in.

Just like workaholics tend to be perfectionistic when it comes to their own job performance, they also tend to hold others to these same standards. Thus, in the workaholic's eyes, nothing is ever good enough. If that workaholic is a supervisor, this can lead to them holding up their employees to unrealistic standards.

Poor delegation. There's a common perception among workaholics that *they* are the only ones who can adequately handle a problem or task, since they hold others' work up to their unreasonably obsessive standards. As a result, they try to manage all responsibilities themselves. This also makes them feel good because it fills all their available time with work. Delegating does the exact opposite: it frees up their time, which is undesirable to them.

While this lack of delegation may feel good for the workaholic leader, it ends up backfiring and hurting the team. If a leader fails to delegate, this creates dependency instead of empowerment. Good leaders provide their employees with opportunities for empowerment, where they can develop and showcase their skills and abilities and come up with unique and creative ideas, all of which improves their self-confidence in their ability to perform their jobs effectively.

Poor scoping. We all might be guilty of underestimating how long it will take to do something, but workaholics are particularly bad at this. They estimate project timelines using their "workaholic clock"—which operates on the assumption that any free hours in a day can and should be claimed for the work. Say a project might take twenty hours. You might scope that as four hours over five days, then add padding and say it can be delivered in seven business days. A workaholic sees an opportunity to do as much of those twenty hours of work as possible as soon as possible—possibly in one go and possibly over the weekend. They may estimate that accounting for commutes and sleep (and little else) they can get the job done in two days. That may be true for them, but it's unhealthy and likely will lead to subpar work (as well as driving all the other unhealthy effects of workaholism on them and their families).

This type of thinking becomes extremely problematic when colleagues are involved (they have not signed up for your timeline) or when the scoping is client-facing. Promising a one-week delivery to a client may excite them, while the workaholic's colleagues or subordinates will know it's an unrealistic timeline. Even worse, the workaholic will often expect and push others to meet these shortened timelines because "it's already been promised to the client," or it's an important customer, critical project, and so forth. And there always seems to be another important client or critical project right around the corner. Rinse, then repeat.

Catastrophizing. Because a workaholic often operates in fight-or-flight mode, their body is constantly in a state of crisis. Think about a time when you were really stressed out about something, and how it affected your demeanor. Maybe you found yourself overly critical of your spouse or children; maybe you were shorter with your colleagues or reacted in a more negative way than you should have to what in retrospect was a relatively benign comment. When we are in crisis mode, we tend to impose our crisis on those around us, particularly when we work with or lead others.

. . .

Workaholism, it can be said, negatively affects work performance. Let me reiterate that workaholics are *not* the most productive workers (even though many of them will tell you they are). Time spent at work, or thinking about work, or being busy—these are poor indicators of quality of performance.

But ironically, although workaholism is not related to good performance, I have found in my research that it *is* related to managerial status. For all of what we've just gone over—the bad health outcomes, the damaging effect on families, the difficulty working with colleagues—companies still reward workaholics with promotions because of what they *seem* to be. Organizations, just like people, misconstrue busyness as productivity. They reward the "first one in, last one out" despite the fact that we know those metrics mean little to good results. They celebrate the always-working mindset even as it drives workers into sickness and depression.

Rewarding workaholic behaviors hurts organizations. It reinforces a culture of workaholism by showing that those who obsess about work are rewarded for it. And it creates problems with burnout, morale, and engagement by putting people in charge who will have unrealistic expectations of what others can and should do. Overall, this enabling of the workaholic hurts both the individual and the organizational performance.

Are you enabling workaholism? The next chapter will help you find out.

Key Takeaways

In this chapter, you learned about the impact of workaholism on the workaholic, their families, and the people they work with, as well as how and why workaholism is linked to these negative outcomes.

- Workaholic behavior includes constant rumination about work, taking on too much, always doing, and perfectionism.

- Workaholics are always operating in fight-or-flight mode.

- Workaholics do not take the time to properly recover from work.

- Workaholism is linked to an increased risk of heart disease, weakened autoimmune responses, poor sleep, negative emotions, and potential to fuel other addictions.

- Women may face even more detrimental consequences of workaholism than men.

- Workaholism affects our families by increasing marital tension, increasing the burden on partners, and straining relationships with children.

- Workaholics negatively affect their own performance and the performance of others at work.

CHAPTER 3

Kicking the Habit

If you had to relive a single day in your life, what would it be?

This was the question posed to me by our industrial-organizational psychology graduate students. (They had recently started a new tradition of quizzing their professors at the beginning of each class.) I told them that the day I'd like to relive was the birth of my daughter. "'How sweet,' you all must be thinking," I told them. "'She wants to cherish how special that moment was for her and her family.' I could lie and say 'Sure, yeah, that's it.' But the real reason I want to relive this day is because I'd like to be able to experience the joy of her birth. I didn't enjoy it because I was a workaholic."

Alex was born three years into my PhD program, smack in the middle of midterms. I was at the coffee shop on the afternoon before, scrambling to complete a take-home midterm when my contractions started. Not wanting to stop my work, I told myself I would continue until the contractions were consistent. That bought me several more hours. I pushed it as far as I physically could—too far, probably, as I shouldn't have been working at all—until the pain was unbearable and the contractions were consistent, at which point I reluctantly stopped my work and headed home (and shortly thereafter to the hospital).

My memories of that day, and the days following Alex's birth, should have been about the experience of labor, the joy of childbirth, and the building of a family. I was instead filled with anxiety and panic over the fact that I hadn't finished my midterm, which I forced myself to return to within seventy-two hours. The next week was a blur of sleepless nights and feverish work when I could muster the energy. The week after Alex was born was spring break, and I got a classmate to cover my class the following week, but after that two-week "break," I went right back to my classes and teaching obligations. Why, I ask myself now, did I not request a substitute for my class for the rest of the semester, or an extension on my coursework? How could I have been so invested in work when I had a literal newborn at home, mere hours old?

Today, I still carry guilt over the fact that I prioritized work over my daughter during those first few months of her life.

Because of my research, I know that my story is not unique, unfortunately. Many of the individuals I interviewed recounted similar feelings of guilt and regret once they had realized they were workaholics. Take Gabe, for instance. Gabe is the founder and CEO of a tech company. He recalled how his "aha!" moment came when he was watching a touching scene at the end of the movie *The Notebook*, when the husband is holding his wife's hand and saying he wants to be with her until the end, and it hit Gabe that he loved to work more than he loved his family. He wept. For Gabe, that scene was deeply emotional and impactful as he came to the realization that although he was a provider for his wife and kids, he was spending more time and attention on his work than he was on his relationships with them. "I've shared that moment of realization with people," he told me. "It's sad and embarrassing, but it produced the desperation for me to change."

Perhaps you have had a similar experience when something caused you to stop and reexamine your priorities. For many, the Covid-19 pandemic was that moment—when the whole world was brought to a standstill and our health and safety superseded our immediate work deadlines. Perhaps a devastating medical diagnosis or death of a loved one woke you up. Many I have spoken with only had that "aha!" moment after a serious health scare. Indeed, this is what opened author and businesswoman Arianna Huffington's eyes, when she collapsed and broke her cheekbone out of exhaustion due to overwork across eighteen-hour days.[1]

In this chapter, I'm going to walk you through several activities and exercises that may be helpful in identifying workaholic behavior and beginning to mitigate it. I've found these activities particularly effective especially for people who sense they have a problem but don't know how to begin. I've also found that even small improvements tend to have an outsized and lasting impact. Once people start dealing with their workaholism, like I did, they want to keep finding ways to prevent it from creeping back in.

These activities are also useful to bring to someone you are concerned about. Or, if you manage people in an organization, you can bring these activities into your employee resources.

Awareness Activities

Activity 1: Reflect on Your Current and Future Self

If you are worried that you or someone you know is a workaholic, self-reflection is a good place to start dealing with it. Of course, it must be honest self-reflection, and it should center on how your (or the person's) behavior may be affecting you and those around you. Ask questions such as:

- Are my work hours sustainable?

- Is my work behavior affecting my health?

- How often am I bringing work home or thinking about work when I am supposed to be doing something else?

- Am I able to fully disengage from my work without giving into temptations to check my work email "one last time" that day?

- Are there times when I regret missing an important event for my child or partner due to my work?

Write down answers to these questions. Be honest. It's so easy to have a knee-jerk reaction—"Nah, my health is fine"—as a defense mechanism or to rationalize behavior, just like alcoholics saying, "I can stop drinking if I need to." Ask others about your answers. Do they agree? If you answered yes to any of these, it will help to admit it, and to even say it out loud: "I can't sustain these hours," or "I check my email constantly after 11 p.m."

And if you feel regret about missing things due to work, you are not alone. According to Bronnie Ware, author of *The Top Five Regrets of the Dying*, the number two regret of people on their deathbed is "I wish I hadn't worked so hard." The number one regret: "I wish I'd had the courage to live a life true to myself, not the life others expected of me."[2] So ask yourself, What is really important to you? Are you living in line with these values?

Industrial-organizational psychologist Dr. Lauren Kuykendall recommends another reflection activity, which she calls *making your future self relatable*. Picture yourself at a specific point in the future, say five, ten, or even twenty years from now. Think about your life as it stands now and imagine the specific implications of your current choices, behaviors, and decisions on your future self. It's easy, Dr. Kuykendall tells me, to make decisions on what feels better right now, in the moment. As humans, we tend to place greater value on short-term rewards and gains and discount the value of rewards that may not come until a later point in time—a phenomenon called *time discounting*.[3] However, your future self may greatly benefit from decisions you make today that will support you down the road.

For example, I asked Alan, a veterinary technician, to indulge me in this activity, focusing on his ten-years-in-the-future self. I asked him questions about what his life would look like then, such as, *What will your job role/title be? Where will you be living? Will you have any pets or kids? How many of each? Will you be married? What are your hobbies? What are your passions? Close your eyes and imagine a day in the life of your future self.* Future Alan would be forty-three, and he would own his own veterinary practice. He said he hoped to be married, no kids, but many pets—three cats and three dogs. He said he'd like to spend a lot of his free time volunteering at the nearby animal sanctuary and hiking—hopefully, with his future husband.

Then, Alan reflected on some of his behaviors now and if they were sustainable to achieve this future vision. He had to admit that he was putting in a lot of hours to build up financial reserves but could feel the physical toll of it. He also acknowledged that, until he was prompted, he rarely thought about those extracurriculars because he mostly thought about work and what he had to do to get ahead at work. He hadn't had a good relationship in some time because work always came first. He could start to see that although workaholic behavior *seemed* like the path to achieving his future self, it was probably going to impede him.

I realize that, as a workaholic overachiever, your first instinct will be to focus on things like money and time spent working, like Alan did. That is, *If I put in long hours now and work all that overtime, I will have more money and get those promotions.* While that may be true, money can't buy you time (remember the biggest regrets of the dying), and you are discounting the costs to you of approaching your work this way—physical and mental health, relationships, and other issues I talked about in previous chapters. Try to focus instead on the most important relationships your future self will have, or your important values and goals. (Also, read the book *Time Smart*, by Ashley Whillans, which can provide you with additional tools to reframe time as a resource even more valuable than money.[4])

Try to paint a vivid picture of your future self, focusing on those important relationships and values. To work through my own struggles with workaholism, I tried this activity, focusing on my relationship with my two kids, who are so important to me. My youngest is currently in middle school. That means that in about five years, neither kid will likely be living at home anymore. In five years, most likely my kids and I will no longer be physically a part of each other's daily lives. I picture future Malissa on her weekly phone call with each of her kids. My friend and his parents talk on the phone every Friday at noon. I imagine myself having a similar tradition. Maybe I'll integrate this phone call into one of my walks. I also would like to establish a yearly family vacation, at least until each child has a family of their own or can afford their own vacations. I start jotting down some cool spots we could go to as a family in future years—Italy, Hawaii, Alaska, somewhere to see the Northern Lights.

It is my hope and dream that my future self will have a close bond with my children long after they've flown the nest. So, what are the little (or big) things I can do *today* to increase the chances that we will have a close relationship well into their adulthood?

Workaholics tend to fall into the time-discounting trap, prioritizing "urgent" work tasks over other obligations. However, because workaholics are always putting out fires, there never ceases to be something that will supersede other obligations. Our prioritization of work over all unintentionally diminishes the things in our life that need our attention—our spouse, parents, pets, children. Before we know it, we are the overly busy, inattentive dad in Harry Chapin's classic song "Cat's in the Cradle." Five or ten years into the future, we're strangers to our loved ones.

OK, you've pictured yourself in the future. How does that affect your priorities now? Rank order your big-picture priorities and use this list to guide your time.

For example, Alan ranked his big-picture priorities for his future in this order:

1. Establishing a high-quality relationship with his future partner

2. Spending time with his animals

3. Volunteering at the animal sanctuary

4. Hiking and maintaining physical fitness

"I love my work," Alan told me, "but I also realize that it can be an emotionally challenging career and I will need an escape. My other passions can provide that to me." Seeing his priorities on paper helped Alan see that when push comes to shove, his *true* passions and priorities lie outside of work. Having this list might help Alan remember, when he is asked to take on an extra shift at the clinic for the second weekend in a row, that the extra cash he may earn does no good in helping him move toward any of his big-picture priorities.

Activity 2: Record Your Workaholic Patterns

Next, let's take a thorough assessment of how you spend your time. Here's how we do it:

1. Right now (don't wait), open a new "note" on your phone, take out a piece of paper, or open a new file on your computer.

2. Record the day and time.

3. Write down what have you been doing for the past hour. (Presumably reading this book, right?)

4. Now write down any work-related activities you did while doing the things you listed in the previous step. And record notes about any thoughts that popped into your mind during the past hour about work.

5. Finally, record the emotions you felt with each of these work thoughts. If it helps, you can make a template to access with the simple prompts:

> Date/time:
>
> What I've been doing this hour:
>
> Work activities:
>
> Work thoughts:
>
> Feelings:

If you are a workaholic, you'll have thought about work at least a few times, or the activity you're doing will somehow be related to work, even if it's not work time. Typical responses to "What did you think about?" are a work to-do list, some interaction with a colleague, an upcoming deadline, or a big event like a performance review. Typically, these thoughts *intrude*. You don't set out to think about work; it interrupts whatever you're doing. (Your body is craving that work fix that you're addicted to, just like the workaholics we met in earlier chapters who felt physical nausea in the pit of their stomach, when they were separated from work.)

If you were honest in recording your feelings, you'll typically notice that you wrote down that you were feeling guilty or anxious or irritated that other things were preventing you from working. You may have felt dread about being judged an underperformer or fear that you'd be noticed for not putting in as much work as others or as expected. For me, any time I think about an important work deadline, or even just my weekly or daily to-do list (for example, getting a draft of this chapter to my editor!), my stomach begins to hurt—that pit-of-your-stomach feeling. I start to feel dread and a little panic.

Once you've done this assessment, there's one more step. Set an alarm on your phone for another non-work time in the next day or two. When the alarm goes off, open the note file and repeat the process. Do this over some workdays and some weekends. Each time it goes off, take out your journal and fill in your notes. Keep up this journal activity until you have about ten of these entries. Looking at the cumulative list, do you notice any patterns? This can help you identify if you are having workaholic thoughts and feelings and the frequency with which you are experiencing them. Feel free to supplement the list with other salient times when you were not at work but had a strong work-related urge or thought.

Sandra (we met her in chapter 2) found it very cathartic to keep this simple journal. It was through recording her negative work thoughts that she was able to pinpoint that her biggest struggles were that she always felt like she had to be going at full speed at work and that everything she did (even non-work things) had to be perfect. To counteract her feelings of being overwhelmed, Sandra has prioritized her mental and physical well-being through healthy tools that she learned from Workaholics Anonymous. She focuses on improving in four areas: delegating more, lowering her performance standards for herself, pacing herself, and improving her prioritization. It's a practice that takes a lot of work but is helping her beat back her workaholic tendencies.

. . .

Hopefully, the exercises above will help you to become more aware of your workaholic thoughts and feelings. From now on, when you catch yourself having these thoughts, practice calling them out. Say to yourself, either aloud or in your head, "I am having workaholic urges right now." Or "These are workaholic thoughts and emotions." By naming the workaholic urges, thoughts, and behaviors, you are doing what psychiatrist Dr. Dan Siegel calls "name it to tame it."[5] Research shows that labeling our emotions and feelings can signal to the brain to send soothing neurotransmitters and physically calm us and start the process of recovering.

Counteracting Workaholic Behavior

OK, now that you have done these activities, hopefully you have built awareness of your values, priorities, and workaholic tendencies. Now you can start targeting some of the behaviors with specific steps.

We're going to focus on six strategies: redefining "urgent"; reinventing the to-do list; learning to say no and delegate; fixing the workaholic clock; controlling the rumination; and embracing rest and recovery.

Redefining "Urgent"

What percentage of your to-do list is urgent? If you have workaholic tendencies, I suspect it's most of it. What's more, I suspect that if you stacked up all the items on your to-do list in some kind of rank order, most of the top items are work-related. Maybe you don't even put non-work items on your list.

Making everything high priority puts you in a kind of crazy busy mode. Workaholics Anonymous's *Book of Discovery* calls this "frantic multitasking."[6] Many people I've spoken with talk about how they almost feel addicted to the adrenaline they feel when they are in this "mode." No better way to create a mini-crisis than to assign everything as urgent.

The problem is, this means we put ourselves and our bodies in constant fight-or-flight mode, which significantly increases our stress. In fact, Dr. Darria Long, author of the bestseller *Mom Hacks*, notes that research shows that people who cannot differentiate threat from non-threat (everything is urgent!) have double the levels of stress hormones of those who can.[7]

Remember Lauren, the former academic and member of Workaholics Anonymous whose workaholism fueled her dependence on alcohol? She recalled one vacation, stopping by a grocery store so she could pick up a cake for a family party. She got the cake but then found herself standing in the hot parking lot while her husband waited in the car with crying children. The cake was melting in the summer sun. And "I'm having this conversation with this new study coordinator. I called her to make sure that she was doing things right. Remembering all the little details."

"It felt urgent," Lauren says. "And it felt like things were going to spiral out of control and somehow be a reflection on me if I wasn't there." It was so urgent that she interrupted her vacation, ruined a cake, and made her family miserable so she could initiate the call with this person—who, by the way, didn't appreciate being micromanaged.

What was this urgent matter with the study coordinator? "I can't even remember what it was."

Workaholics struggle with prioritization. Remember Ivy, the retired lab technician and llama ranch manager. When her therapist asked her, "Well, what *are* your priorities?" it stumped her. Eventually she said, "I'm not supposed to have priorities. I'm just supposed to get it all done." Likewise, Gabe told me that before he was able to get a handle on his workaholism, "everything was on the same level. Everything was important. Everything was urgent."

It was only after he faced his workaholism head on that he could see that this mentality fostered great fear and anxiety—Gabe called himself "a big fear machine. . . . And no one is successful when a big fear machine is in charge," he said. "My constant fear of failing fostered an extremely negative environment for everyone working around me." According to Gabe, people could feel the fear and anxiety that his sense of urgency with *everything* created. They could read in his emails how every matter was top priority. They could hear urgency in his voice. Frantic, frazzled, hurried. And because everything was urgent, he struggled to let things go that didn't come out as he had hoped. Even when others saw past matters as less important or even trivial, he stayed backward-focused: *Why did the company do this? Why was this action taken instead of that one?*

Now that he's recovering, Gabe can see how treating everything as urgent not only held him back but also held back his company and those working for him: "It was very chaotic."

As part of his process now, he has redefined what "urgent" is and allows only a few items to rise to that level. That means focusing on the five or six big-ticket items that he does every two weeks—that's it. He doesn't allow himself more. It's not always easy, but sometimes the brute force of setting artificial restrictions is a good way to redefine your relationship with work and begin to see "urgent" in a new light.

Another way to help you see that not everything is as urgent as it probably seems to you, the workaholic, is to do retroactive reviews of tasks. Look at a list of things that were on your to-do list, say, a month ago, and think about how important they seem now in retrospect. Ask others what they think, too. You may realize that what was driving the urgency around some tasks wasn't their actual importance, but your workaholic reflex to treat any unfinished work as urgently needing to be completed (and perfectly!). But looking back, you may see that the task didn't matter all that much or didn't need to be completed perfectly in that time frame. Keep notes on these tasks and try to spot them when they arise again and assign a lower priority to them.

For example, you may catalog a list of ten urgent tasks from the previous month. One item—an analysis you did for another team about a business opportunity—was urgent for you. You had to show them you had the goods and could get the work to them right away. So you cranked out the analysis in one long night. But one month later, it still hasn't been used by that team. What's more, if they do use it, it will only be for background in a presentation about a potential long-term strategy. What you thought was urgent wasn't urgent at all. The next time a similar request comes up, force yourself to critically question if it's actually a priority.

Another way to redefine "urgent" is to assign a fixed number of non-work items to the top of your to-do list. Pin them so they can't be removed. These could be efforts to prioritize yourself and your health. It may seem simple, but to the always-on work-aholic, it may not be. Literally set simple priorities, like "Eat a healthy snack." Or "Drink lots of water" or "Take restroom breaks." "Sleep." As I type this, I am reminded of my interview with Ivy. On the day I was to interview her, it was a hectic morn-ing, and I forgot to eat lunch. Really, I didn't forget . . . I was hungry, but I didn't eat. I prioritized work over lunch. It got to be 2 p.m., and I hadn't eaten since breakfast. And since I hadn't made time earlier, I knew I wouldn't be able to eat the spring rolls I had heated up until after the interview. Ivy told me she used to tell herself she needed to finish some task before she would go to the bathroom or eat lunch; sometimes this would take her hours to get done, and all the while she was hungry and needing to pee. I couldn't help but laugh, and sheepishly told her that I was certainly not setting a good example at this moment. "Please," she said. "Eat your spring rolls." This was a small moment, but it was meaningful. I really needed to be making some of my work to-dos less urgent and my personal to-dos more urgent. Later that night, my son and I were play-ing our nightly game of ping-pong (something we'd been doing for several months), and I said, "Let's play an extra couple of games tonight." I think the realization during the interview was a good prompt to redefine "urgent" in my life.

Reinventing the To-Do List

There's nothing wrong with to-do lists per se. But in the wrong hands, they can become reinforcers of workaholism. For the work-aholic, a to-do list becomes an invitation to overwork.

The appeal of a to-do list is only partially its structure-giving nature. It's as much about anticipating (and then getting) the satisfaction of checking things off the list. I am one of those people who like to handwrite to-do lists because they feel real physical satisfaction crossing the items off (now some apps have attempted to recreate this experience digitally). And for good reason: research shows that accomplishing a goal can give us a burst of dopamine, we feel positive emotions, and we are motivated to keep working toward accomplishing another goal.[8] I don't know about you, but I've even added tasks I've already completed to my list, just so I can cross them off. There's something very satisfying about getting something *done*.

However, the stark reality is that to-do lists are never going to be fully completed. For the workaholic, *they are self-reinforcing*. For Lauren, the workaholic who talked about her experience with the melting cake on vacation, checking things off on her to-do list was not a satisfying event. It was a problem. "I thought that doing more was going to help," she said. "Because the more I did, the more consumed I was." In other words, crossing things off the list drove her to add more to the list.

This has been found in scientific research even with non-workaholics. In one study, researchers found that when people had high workloads, they *wanted* to take a break. However, those workloads also prevented these people from acting on their desires. Participants were much less likely to take a break when they felt a strong desire to "get it over with" or to reduce the amount of work still needed to be done.[9] Something that can be checked off today leaves one less thing to do tomorrow—theoretically.

Now imagine the same scenario for a workaholic, who sees the high workload as a positive. They don't even want to take a break, even if their bodies are telling them they need it. The whole point is to have work, so the drive to ensure more work by adding to the list outweighs any satisfaction from completing a task. To the workaholic, a break is a signal that something's wrong. A to-do list that gets shorter is a *threat* that triggers a need to fill the empty space.

You can break this pattern, though, by reinventing your to-do list and its purpose. The key is to transform it into a document in which completion of a task is not part of the criteria for what's on the list. There is no focus on finishing what's on the list. There's no crossing off. Instead, you use your to-do lists as a method for *mapping* and *prioritizing,* but not holding yourself accountable for accomplishing everything on the list.

One way to do this is to revisit your to-do lists using the Eisenhower matrix.[10] Also known as the *urgent versus important* matrix, this tool helps individuals identify what tasks they may be spending too much (or too little) time on.

The easiest way to do this is to just take your to-do list, which is probably a linear set of bullet points or numbered items, and place all its items on the matrix seen in figure 3-1.

For example, I thought about everything on my plate this upcoming week and filled them into my own grid, as seen in figure 3-2.

In the high-importance/high-urgency category is getting the next draft of this chapter to my editor. Also important, but lower

FIGURE 3-1

The Eisenhower matrix

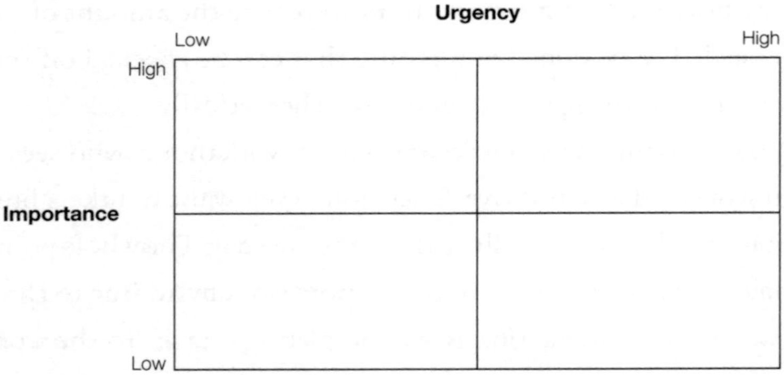

FIGURE 3-2

Matrix with to-do items

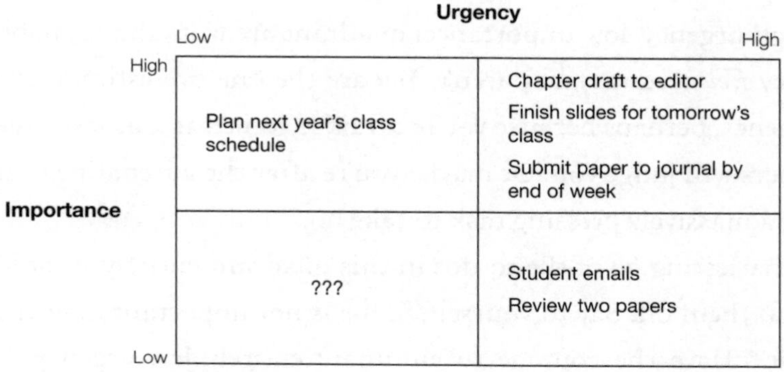

urgency, is planning next semester's schedule for the psychology department—I know I have a couple of weeks to do that, but it's an important part of my job as associate head. Answering emails from students typically would fall in the high-urgency but low-importance category. I have two papers to review as a member of various editorial boards, and I would place them there. I also have two action editor letters, and I would place them in that category as well. I had a tough time identifying things that would fall in the low-urgency and low-importance quadrant—a sign of my workaholic tendencies perhaps. If anything, maybe these are the to-do list fillers that I would add to my list right after I complete them simply for the gratification of checking them off.

This reimagined mapping of the to-do list is going to be hard at first. That's because for the workaholic, almost everything will end up in the top right quadrant. Everything is urgent and important! If anything, creating this view only reinforces those feelings of having to complete everything and getting a knot in the pit of your stomach if you identified items that didn't land in the top right.

It will take effort to *not* put everything in the top right quadrant; I still struggle with that. But if you can force yourself to map with some self-reflection and honesty, overcoming those innate feelings of all work being all-important, you can start to let go of some tasks. For example, things that fall in the bottom right (high urgency, low importance) quadrant are workaholic enablers. They *feel* necessary but aren't. *You* are the one overestimating the urgency, perhaps because you're afraid if you treat it as less urgent, others will judge you. Or maybe you're after the adrenaline of having a massively pressing task to take on.

Try letting go of the to-dos in this quadrant entirely, or at least push them off. Say to yourself, "This is not important now. It can wait." Have the courage to eliminate entirely low-urgency, low-importance to-dos (if you even have any) and learn to respect but not address high-importance, low-urgency items (top left). Those are future plans. Again, tell yourself, "Those can wait."

Equally important, make sure you force yourself to put to-dos on the list that are not about work at all. If you are intent on resetting your life and escaping workaholism, you should have at least one high-urgency, high-importance task that isn't work-related at all. When it came to Gabe's daily to-do lists, he found himself most effective when he created a daily action plan where he charted out his activities on an hourly (and sometimes even half-hourly) basis based on urgency and importance. And at the top of that action plan was time to focus on his health—not work! In his top right quadrant is "Exercise." Today, it's common for Gabe to schedule rock-climbing sessions two days a week in the middle of his workday, for example.

There are other ways to reinvent the to-do list. In her TED talk, *An ER Doctor on Triaging Your "Crazy Busy" Life*, Dr. Darria Long uses an emergency room triage model to recategorize to-dos. Red is immediately life-threatening. Yellow is serious, but not immediately life-threatening. Green is minor. There's one other category: black, which means no measures can save the patient.[11]

Applying this to a to-do list—again, with discipline and honesty—forces you to make decisions about what is truly important, rather than treating everything as urgent. Answering an email from a frantic student who is asking for a last-minute meeting the day before a paper is due or responding to a high-maintenance client who sends an email, then follows up with a phone call and text twenty minutes later, will feel highly urgent and highly important to a workaholic. They go to the top of the to-do list and create discomfort until they're crossed off. But with a triage system, you assess if this is truly a code red. You ask yourself questions about the implications of not completing the task immediately, or at all. These could be code yellow since, while they're loud and distracting, they can wait and don't need to be done perfectly. As with a matrix, the key is to force yourself to make sure every category has some tasks in it. Not everything can be a code red. And as with the matrix, you can mix in tasks that are meant to separate you from work in healthy way. If Gabe had used triage, for example, he could have put "Schedule rock climbing this week" in his red category while pushing down some less urgent work tasks into yellow or green.

Author Adam Grant has learned to focus less on doing everything and more on prioritization with his own unique method.[12] For a long time, he thought he wanted to optimize everything, and that would be the secret to getting everything done. But the process of trying to optimize his time exposed to him how much time he was wasting, which frustrated him. And then he was faced with trying to manage his emotions about how frustrated he was with his time management. But whereas Gabe focuses on a few things over two weeks, Grant likes to set different horizons. He starts the day with a clear idea of what projects matter to him. And ideally, he does this at a week level and even month level: *What projects are going to get my best time and energy?* And then if he focuses on those, he finds he doesn't worry as much about how he spends his time. And he knows he is moving forward on his main priority.

It can't be stressed enough that whatever items you put on these alternatives to the simple to-do list, they're not meant to be finished. Crossing stuff off isn't the end game. Instead, they are meant to give you a view into what you see as what needs to get done and serve as a forcing function for taking the active step of deprioritizing some things. Through experience, you will see that even though you deprioritized some work task, the sky didn't fall when you didn't complete it right away, or perfectly, or even complete it at all.

Learning to Say No and Delegate

Workaholics tend to be poor delegators. The drive to always have work to do means they'd rather take on work themselves than give it to someone else. They don't say no to requests because it feels *good* to be asked to do work. And their need for tasks to be done more perfectly means they can't trust others to do the work to their standards. Sandra, a government analyst and member of Work-aholics Anonymous (we met her in chapter 2), describes how her workaholic tendencies were exacerbated by one of her old bosses' own workaholism. He would overcommit the unit. Sandra recalls that because of his inability to say no, he became the go-to for any assignment that others didn't want because it was too challenging or the timeline was clearly unrealistic. Because he couldn't say no, she told me, her team was always expecting another assignment to get dumped into their laps at any moment. At any time, another assignment could potentially throw everything into chaos. He would come to her cubicle as soon as he was done with an impor-tant meeting with a frantic look in his eye. It wasn't long before he dumped the assignment on the team because he was anxious to get started on it right away. This pattern led to Sandra eventually bottoming out as a workaholic.

To overcome this predisposition takes practice. In his podcast, *WorkLife with Adam Grant,* Grant talks about how he practices saying no more often than he is inclined to. He does it by setting priorities that may echo some of the triage and matrix methods for your to-do list mentioned in the previous section. Here's how he describes his method:

- Who to help? Family first, students second, colleagues third, everyone else fourth.

- When to help? At designated times that didn't interfere with my goals.

- And how to help? In areas where I had a unique contribution to make.

And, he adds, "now, when people reach out with requests that stretch beyond my wheelhouse or my calendar, I refer them to relevant resources: an article or an expert."[13]

I can attest to the fact that Grant does practice what he preaches. When I asked to interview him for this book, he politely said he was on sabbatical and pointed me to the exact podcast episode I just referenced. Also, I had already had some of these conversations about workaholism with Grant when I interviewed him the year before, so I had some good material for the book already. Well done, Adam. A workaholic would have, without hesitation, interrupted their packed schedule (first of all, they wouldn't be on sabbatical, but if they were, they'd be working during it) to speak to me, putting me right at the top of the overlong to-do list. They'd gather resources for me and offer to follow up. If Grant has workaholic tendencies, he's managing them well.

When Gabe realized the importance of delegation, it completely transformed his role within his company and allowed him to focus on what brought value while handing off other tasks to people more suited to them. This is a hard thing for a workaholic to do— it's giving away work. Gabe's unlikely inspiration to try came from his favorite football team. "I'm a big Eagles fan, and reading about their GM, I saw he was not well liked by Eagles fans because he's been a very poor drafter. But he's so good in a few other areas. He's great at salary cap analysis and trades and free agency evaluation. Someone made this point, and I realized that was me. I'm really good at a few things in my job and I'm terrible with a few things, but I'm trying to do it all. So I came back and started to change my role and step away from the day-to-day, and we shaped a COO role."

The results are what helped workaholic Gabe stick with it. He noticed that once he gathered the fortitude to try to do less, it was a positive change, so he worked at sticking with it.

After success on her journey to combat her workaholism, Veronica (the psychotherapist in private practice who has been able to successfully manage her workaholic tendencies in her paid job and in her passion projects) began helping her friend who was a CEO of a large and unwieldy company. This CEO was burned out and copped to Veronica that she felt exhausted, her health was suffering, and she felt she needed to quit.

Veronica helped her friend try a different strategy—massive amounts of delegation and learning to say no. Together, they brainstormed what she could do differently within the system. She was not utilizing the expertise of her assistants, who had untapped and incredibly advanced skills in some areas where her friend struggled. But she hadn't learned this because, like many workaholics, she hadn't trusted others with work and didn't like the idea of saying no to taking on new work.

When Veronica's friend forced herself to learn to delegate, she learned of her assistants' deeply underutilized skill sets, and the transformation has been astounding. She went from seventy-hour workweeks and an unhealthy work obsession to fewer than thirty hours. Her employees appreciate the healthy behavior modeling, and the company hasn't suffered just because she's working less. Meanwhile her assistants have blossomed under their boss's new-found trust and delegation to them.

Fixing the Workaholic Clock

Workaholics tend to underestimate how long it will take to do something, so they overcommit to too many things in too short a time. This is the *workaholic clock* error that leads to so many problems—not only for the workaholic but for others who are pulled into projects and tasks that have been set on an unreasonable timeline.

In fact, everyone, to some degree, underestimates the amount of time it will take to complete a task—it's a phenomenon known as the *planning fallacy*.[14] But, workaholics are particularly bad at it because of the adrenaline high they get from having urgent work to complete. It's like their brain is saying, *I want that work. Say whatever time frame you need to get it.* And unlike others who may simply fall behind on unreasonable deadlines, workaholics are much more likely to do anything they can physically do to try to meet them.

To reset the workaholic clock, you must acknowledge your clock is off, and then gauge how far it's off. This will take some practice and careful note-taking. You can do two things. First, review a few projects that were crashes with a non-workaholic colleague. Look at the budgeted time and then take an honest assessment of what that time budget should have been. Say you budgeted a week, but your colleague thinks realistically it was a three-week job. Make note of that. Then, for the next week, before you start any task, write down the amount of time you *think* it will take you. I did this today for a letter of recommendation I had to write. I jotted down twenty minutes as my estimate. I made a note of when I started and finished. Thirty-five minutes. OK, not terrible. Then I tried it with something more difficult: get the next round of edits of this chapter to my editor. This should take me about five more hours. Given that I wasn't going to do it in one sitting, it required some more careful note-taking. So every time I dived in, I noted the time, and when I finished, I noted that too. I then put those times into a spreadsheet.

By the time I felt the edits were good enough to send off, the total number of hours was 13.5. Ouch. More than double what I thought it would take. I did this for a few more projects and found that my average actual time spent was usually about 1.8 times my original estimate.

All right, that's step one, but the task is not complete. I also had to account for the number of hours I expect to work in a given day compared with others. This is particularly important if you are a boss and setting deadlines for your team. For example, I expect a task will take twenty hours, but I know I tend to take 1.8 times my estimated time. My first calculation tells me I need thirty-six hours for the task (20 hours × 1.8 workaholic clock = 36 hours). A workaholic might look at that number and say, "OK, about two-and-a-half days of work," because they expect to put in fourteen-hour days.

Instead, you must force yourself to budget the time on a non-workaholic schedule. Either extend the deadline by a few days or bring in a few more team members to help lighten everyone's load.

Controlling the Rumination

As with other afflictions, at the core of workaholism is something you could consider positive—a passion for something. It's the inability to throttle that passion, to turn it off, that becomes the issue. Passion becomes all-consuming obsession—to the point that the workaholic actively seeks out ways to fuel the obsession.

As with me, it has taken Adam Grant practice and it still takes willpower for him *not* to work. He once referred to me as a "meta workaholic" trying to apply my obsessive work habits to study obsessive work habits in a way that would allow me to work a little bit less. (He noted how ironic it was that two workaholics were in part dealing with their affliction by putting the study of work at the center of their lives.) We talked about friends who were not like us, serious procrastinators who struggle with trying to figure out how to avoid the next Netflix binge or YouTube distractions. For us it takes willpower *not* to work. Grant has to force himself not to engage in the next task.

If he notices he's ruminating about work—thinking about it while trying to enjoy family time, or propping open a laptop while watching TV, or feeling stress, anxiety, or guilt about not working—he forces himself to stop. He will ask himself why he feels that. He has some questions and statements he'll repeat to himself: "Who said I should be working every minute? I don't even have a boss!" "What is the point of having tenure if I don't get to decide for myself how many hours I will be spending on which projects?"

Rumination is in some ways one of the hardest workaholic tendencies to combat because it's one of the most internal. It happens in a place—your mind—where no one sees it, and it's hard to control. Thoughts and feelings come whether you want them to or not. And what you feel may be quite different from what the world sees. For example, I asked Grant how he was able to juggle all his activities: his full-time job as a professor at Wharton, his speaking engagements, consulting, hosting a podcast, and writing many books. "Tell me your secrets," I eagerly asked him. "How are you able to do all of this?

To that, Grant answered, "The truth is, I don't feel productive. On a daily basis, I'm falling behind my goals for how much I want to get done."

Even now, as successful and as thoughtful as he is about controlling his workaholic tendencies, Grant (and I, if I'm being honest) must work with our rumination.

It's key to understand that you won't be able to simply eliminate the rumination. You have to learn to listen to it and work with it. Grant has his mantras that he repeats to himself. You may also write down some of those to take out and read aloud when you feel the rumination getting to be too much. It may be something as simple as "This work can wait. I need downtime to recover." Find the mantra that keeps the rumination at bay for you. Practice all the mindfulness techniques you can and find one that fits, whether it's meditation, breathing exercises, or something else. Learn to work with your mind.

Here's another tip: *Schedule your ruminating thoughts for later.*

For example, if I catch myself thinking about the project at night, I reschedule the thought by saying, "No, Malissa. Not tonight. How about you schedule an hour in the morning tomorrow to think about it instead?" Then, I make myself an action plan for two to three specific steps I will take for that project.

This helps to counteract the *Zeigarnik effect*—a phenomenon where unfulfilled goals tend to persist in the mind.[15] Even by taking a few minutes at the end of the workday to plan where, when, and how you will accomplish your unfulfilled goals from that day has been shown to increase individuals' ability to detach from their work at the end of the workday—particularly for those with high workloads and low self-control.[16]

It also helps to control ruminating if you remind yourself of good outcomes from working less. For Veronica, her pay and hours were directly related to the number of patients she saw, so she was terrified that no one would come to her again if she raised rates to lower her workload. But they came. And she raised rates again, and they kept coming. If she's ruminating about not working enough, she can calm herself by saying "I raised rates before, and people still came. I have a waiting list for patients now. I don't need to work more."

Workaholics often tell themselves they can't stop working so long and hard because their students, patients, clients, or customers count on them. They use a fear of letting other people down as a driver. It can help to talk to some of those people. Ask them if they will feel let down if you put in a little less time or stop communicating with them after hours. My experience with workaholics is they are surprised at how *relieved* these people are that you're taking the step to adjust.

Embracing Rest and Recovery

As I discussed in the chapter 2, our bodies are not physically able to remain in constant fight-or-flight mode. Part of a healthy stress response is the eventual calming down of our regulatory systems, which allows us to return to homeostasis. We can help our bodies reset and recover spent energy while we are awake, as well as through sleep. Research definitively shows when we rest and engage in recovery activities, we have better well-being, *particularly* when we have a lot on our plates.[17]

Many workaholics are so caught up in the fight-or-flight response that even sleep becomes "a nuisance" and "a waste of time." Those are real descriptions of sleep I've heard from workaholics, who seem almost annoyed that sleep can't be somehow engineered out of their lives. Workaholics tend to survive on less sleep than they need, until their bodies start fighting back.

We all know that sleep is important. Research has taught us this. However, as burnout management coach Emily Ballesteros put it to me, "The only time you rest should not be when you are dead asleep. You have to have rest in your waking hours."

Sleep is hard enough for workaholics. But rest when they are not sleeping feels doubly foolish because, in their minds, it's not *necessary*. Desea, the kindergarten teacher who described her perfectionist tendencies when it came to organizing her classroom, described unscheduled time as her biggest struggle, a trigger that left her feeling like time was running out and sent her into a full workaholic frenzy.

Of course, research tells us how valuable rest is, and that many assumptions we have about rest are false. For example, resting can be more effective when it's taken *before* you are tired, as opposed to after.[18]

Luckily, there's plenty of research on the myriad ways we can rest and recover from work. I'm going to describe four ways workaholics can adopt rest as a way to combat their tendencies. I will apply concepts from the recovery literature about reducing the strain on our bodies and improving our well-being, as outlined by preeminent scholar Dr. Sabine Sonnentag.[19]

- Psychological detachment. This is a full mental "disconnect" from work. Switching off your work-related thoughts when you are not at work. To facilitate psychological detachment, you want to force yourself to try an activity that is not work-related in which you can shift your attention toward something (or someone) else. Think of activities you may have thought about before but always told yourself you had no time for. If you force yourself to do it, you may become engrossed and detached from work. This could include something like immersing yourself in a good book or TV series, cooking, or catching up with an old friend (but resist the temptation to talk about work).

- Physical activity. Of course, we all know that medical research has shown the positive effects of exercise on our mood and physical health, but it can also help us rest and recover from work, too. And there's lots of research to support its benefits to workers. Recall Gabe, who schedules rock climbing into his workweek. Far from making him a less effective worker, it makes him *better* because he is detaching from work during work hours, while also fueling his energy. Physical activity has been shown to be even more beneficial for workaholics than the average worker; one study found those higher in workaholism tendencies were happier in the evening and felt more recovered the next morning on days in which they exercised or participated in sports after work.[20]

- Relaxation. Meditation or other relaxation exercises such as yoga lower your sympathetic nervous system activation, which brings your heart rate down, helps you breathe more deeply, and relaxes your muscles. It literally takes you out of the fight-or-flight response, reducing stress. Many of the individuals I spoke with from Workaholics Anonymous told me about how they have found ways to relax. Debra, a licensed clinical counselor, talked to me about how she would take a few minutes each morning to practice putting golf balls in her living room or listen to jazz music. She and a friend committed to each other that they would each take two quiet pauses each day, which meant simply pausing and taking three or four slow, deep breaths.

- Mastery experiences. This involves engaging in non-work-related activities that challenge you to learn and grow. Any number of activities can fall into this category. For one of my graduate students, it's woodworking. My editor plays guitar. Others may pursue learning a foreign language, perfecting their baking or gardening skills, or taking up a sport. It could be anything, really. Become the best builder of sandcastles in the world if that works for you.

Adam Grant recalled a frank conversation he had with scholar and collaborator Sabine Sonnentag after they had published a couple of papers together. She told him he wasn't necessarily a great role model for the stuff she studies. He asked her what he did wrong, and she said, "You know, you're not very good at relaxation."

He agreed with her and even noted that he wished he could just outsource sleep, because it feels like a colossal waste of time. And she told him, "Well, if you've read my research carefully, you can also recharge and rest by doing mastery exercises." It hit him that he was not prioritizing things he loved that *did* feel like a "good waste of time," like playing Ultimate Frisbee. And they allowed him to apply more of those mastery activities. They're different from work, but they still allowed him to apply his passion and engagement and—dare I say—mild obsession.

There is no one-size-fits-all recovery experience, and often people use a combination of them.[21] The most important thing is that you decide which seems the most restorative for you, because having control over what you choose to engage in during your leisure time is also related to more positive outcomes.[22]

So if you find yourself recognizing your workaholic tendency to go, go, go, try instead to participate in some other activity that still requires physical movement but is not related to work. Personally, I enjoy working on fixer-upper projects around the house. I also used to play on a coed soccer team. After some injuries, I retired my soccer shoes in exchange for my coaching whistle (for my son's soccer team) for a couple of years. Nowadays, I do a lot of walking. I've timed to perfection the one-mile loop around my neighborhood and make sure I do at least a couple of those loops a day. However, I know myself well enough to know that my mind will immediately wander toward work if I don't also give it something else to focus on. I'll start thinking about additional things to add to this book, or I will start thinking of the to-do list. So I put in my earbuds and listen to a (non-work-related) podcast or audiobook, which often does the trick.

I also encourage you to experiment with freeing up more time during your regular hours (more on this in chapter 4). Schedule in exercise, rest, mastery experiences. Research on exercise during lunch breaks, for example, has shown that people come back after the break with even more vigor to finish out their workday. Then, even more exciting, that increased vigor has been positively related to greater participation in recovery exercises—specifically, relaxation and mastery experiences.[23] So ask yourself, *Is it possible to take more breaks and cut back on hours and be just as (or more) productive?*

Make intentional choices to choose recovery over work. It's OK to do something that you find pleasurable for the pure goal of finding joy.

. . .

Of course, even as you read this, if you're a workaholic, it all probably sounds and feels difficult. The idea of detaching just seems so hard. You might feel a physical reaction at the thought of carving out time in the middle of the day to *not work*.

All of that is normal, which is why you've seen me so many times mention "forcing" yourself to try something, or being open-minded about an alternative approach, and being disciplined and honest with yourself. This stuff takes work. But that work, I promise, pays off and can help you get to a better, healthier place. Many of the people I've told you about so far in these pages were deeply workaholic and have, through these methods, gotten to better places.

Organizations can play a role, too, by developing programs to encourage and *reward* these behaviors. Because, as you're about to find out, your organization may be enabling workaholism, even if you don't realize it.

Key Takeaways

- The first step in kicking workaholic habits is to become aware of your own workaholic tendencies.

- Reflect on who you want to be in the future, focusing on your big-picture priorities and goals.

- Record your workaholic patterns, both when you are working and also when you aren't.

- To combat your workaholic tendencies:

  - Redefine "urgent"

  - Reinvent your to-do list

  - Learn to say no and delegate

  - Fix your workaholic clock

  - Control rumination

  - Embrace rest and recovery

CHAPTER 4

Are You an Enabler?

It should be clear by now that while workaholism affects individuals, it is partly driven by outside forces. Some of these forces—societal ones—are out of the control of any one person or even any one group of people. But other forces—organizational ones—are explicitly in the control of decision-makers. You may resist this and say, as many have said to me when I give talks on this topic, that the responsibility lies with the individual to get themselves together. After all, no one in an organization wants to feel responsible for contributing to one of their workers' depression or illness.

But I can tell you that if you are part of an organization that doesn't actively discourage and combat workaholism, you may well be enabling it. In fact, it's very likely you are enabling workaholics, whether you know it or not. Perhaps you are scoffing, "This researcher has no idea what it's like to work here (or in this industry). It's just the way it *has* to be." If that's the case, I assure you that you're enabling workaholism. The attitude that, to be competitive, we *must* espouse certain values is a significant contributor to the problem. And the worst offenders are the ones who need the most change.

I realize, however, that change is difficult and takes time. I also realize that you are just one piece of the bigger picture. We also need to discuss the broader societal forces and the organizational culture that you are a part of.

This chapter will push you to critically examine your own work patterns and "the way it's done around here." Change involves looking deeply at the underlying culture of the organization to understand its overwork culture and the signals that are being sent to employees.

We'll examine both cultural and organizational drivers of the problem. Keep an eye out for issues that you may recognize from your own organization.

Societal Forces Driving Workaholism

The Impact of the Industrial Revolution

As noted in the introduction, we have more money and more free time than ever, so the increasing rate of workaholism seems paradoxical. But when we take the *really* long view of work, part of the reason for the paradox can be attributed to cultural, economic, political, and labor shifts that took place in the nineteenth century.[1]

Before the advent of factories, many people lived in rural areas and worked on their own land. Not only did the rise of factories change where people lived and worked, it also changed the way many workers were paid as well as the meaning and value of time. The craftsman class (artisans, woodworkers, metalsmiths) were replaced by a working class, and laborers were no longer paid for completing a task but instead wholly dependent on the number of hours worked. As Celeste Headlee notes in her book, *Do Nothing*, the shift to being paid on an hourly basis marked the moment when "time began to equal money."[2] The longer a worker could spend on a factory line, the longer the machines could crank out product, and hence the more money the company made.

The Industrial Revolution also was a time of philosophical changes—most notably the rise of the Protestant work ethic. The Protestant work ethic, amplified by notable figures such as Max Weber, Benjamin Franklin, Henry Ford, and Frederick Douglass in the 1800s and 1900s, clearly spelled out what was desirable and moral—hard work—and what was undesirable and immoral—idleness. "There is nothing good, great, or desirable," Douglass noted in his 1859 speech on the "self-made man," "that does not come by some kind of labor."[3] Celeste Headlee even argues that during this time, the cultural value of hard work began to over-shadow religion. "To many in Henry Ford's time," she notes in *Do Nothing*, "it was more shameful to miss a day at work than to stay home from church."[4] Overall, the message was very clear. To be worthwhile in the eyes of society, the worst thing one could do was waste time on unpaid endeavors. And paid endeavors rose in value with the time spent doing them.

Leisure time wasn't always looked on with so much disdain, however. Prior to our modern capitalist system, holidays and special occasions were celebrated for days and even weeks. Medieval holidays were *explicitly sanctioned* at the societal level—therefore, it was clear to everyone that participation in these holidays was expected and normative. In some ways, it was rewarded. In medieval England, for example, a third of the year was spent on holiday leisure time.[5] Today, many retail organizations celebrate being open for business on Thanksgiving. How many national holidays are officially recognized in the United States? Eleven, or 3 percent of the year. This is in line with many other countries in the OECD.[6] Asian countries with diverse populations and many religions have the most official holidays, both religious and civic, but their numbers pale in comparison to those from precapitalist times.[7] That society simply valued different things.

Working hours grew in accordance with the Industrial Revolution and the rise in capitalism. Eventually, regulations were needed to limit the maximum number of hours workers were expected to work each day.[8] Even some of these rules don't stop the cultural forces that drive overwork. For example, labor laws require employers to offer vacation time, but more than half of Americans don't use the time they are offered.[9]

Many incentive structures are designed in a way that encourages workaholism. Many jobs tie wages to the number of hours worked, including bonuses for overtime work. This is literally sanctioning workaholic behavior: the more you spend time with your work, the more money you'll receive.

Take Tony, for example, a lineman who receives double and even triple overtime pay during storms. It was almost impossible for him to leave this extra money on the table, because it was so lucrative. But it led to the same outcome it leads to for many who end up with a work addiction: "What ends up happening is we all end up working ourselves to the point of exhaustion." He eventually was forced to cut back his hours when he began having panic attacks, which have since subsided. But he still feels the visceral urge to go back to total work devotion, remembering how well it paid. The example of Tony highlights how incentive structures such as this can lead to a new phenomenon—leisure now feels stressful because time has become too (monetarily) valuable. "When people are paid more," notes economist Gary Becker, "they work longer hours because work is so much more profitable than leisure."[10]

Work Devotion Schema

According to sociologist Mary Blair-Loy, societal factors have shaped our shared cultural assumptions of what makes a meaningful and worthwhile life.[11] These assumptions, called *schemas*, are how we make sense of the world. They are frameworks for how we see, filter, and understand what is going on around us. As a society, we have embraced the *work devotion schema* to describe the cultural model of work that defines individuals by their singular devotion to their careers and work. The work devotion schema endorses and idolizes what scholars have dubbed the *ideal worker*—a person who prioritizes the interests of their employer over their own.[12] The ideal worker is someone who puts in long hours in the office, brings work home and frequently works outside of traditional work hours, is constantly available to respond to work requests, and is eager to demonstrate their work devotion by taking on last-minute assignments or work trips—even (and especially) when they conflict with a personal or family obligation. They seemingly do not have competing obligations that might get in the way of their total devotion.

A commercial for the accounting and advising company Marcum epitomizes how we continue to reinforce the ideal worker norm, even in 2023. In the commercial, a confident-looking job applicant is shown in an interview proclaiming, "I was put on Earth to work here. I don't have hobbies. I don't believe in weekends. The only thing I love more than emails and spreadsheets is meetings . . . about emails and spreadsheets." The camera zooms in to reveal a Marcum adviser who was feeding these lines to the applicant through a device in the applicant's ear. The commercial then proclaims, "Ever wonder where the people with all the answers get all the answers?"[13] The take-home message was clear—if you want to land that big job, you need to make it very clear in your interview that you are, indeed, that ideal worker.

How do you know if the work devotion schema is prevalent at your company? It may be as simple as asking the questions, "What do people at our company believe about people who work a lot of hours?" and conversely, "What do people believe about people who work fewer hours?" At Best Buy, posing these two questions to focus groups of employees revealed a strong ideal worker norm.[14] In response to the first question, a majority of employees described people who work a lot of hours in positive ways, noting they were "dedicated," "important," "they go above and beyond," and "they'll get more rewards." When describing those who worked fewer hours, employees used descriptors such as "slackers," "they don't care," "not contributing what they should," "not making themselves available," "not engaged. They need more work," and "not a team player." You'll learn more about the innovative workplace initiative that sought to change Best Buy's ideal worker culture in chapter 5.

The work devotion schema has become so embedded into our society that we no longer question it, and we unthinkingly pass it on. We no longer have jobs—we have careers and callings, and from a young age we are told we should pursue our passions with an unrelenting feverishness and strive to be that ideal worker. Succeeding in a career is a moral imperative, and a singular focus on advancing within that career becomes a way for us to prove our worth.

I get it—a big part of my identity is my career as a professor, and I take an immense amount of pride in what I have done to get to this point in my career. However, I am also aware that I have unwittingly embraced the work devotion schema to define my self-worth in ways that hurt me and those around me, and I'm actively working toward reevaluating that by devoting my time, energy, and passion to the pursuit of a meaningful and fulfilling life *outside* of work.

The thing about these cultural drivers of workaholism is they are deeply ingrained, and they develop and root themselves over long periods of time. Eventually, they become just part of the fabric of society and fundamental to how we view the world. Brigid Schulte, author of *Overwhelmed* and director of the Better Life Lab, told me the problem is so bad that workaholism has essentially become a function of our culture. "We often feel we don't have a choice because of the cultural narrative that we must always be busy and productive. Feeling bad or guilty when you're not working is not only a marker of workaholism—but I would argue a lot of Americans feel that." Larissa Barber, who studies work recovery, echoes this sentiment in our conversation. "It's culturally OK to say, 'I'm busy and I'm overloaded,' but it's not OK to say things like 'I had family obligations,' especially if you are a woman." What ends up happening, Barber says, is that because everyone uses the "busy" excuse, we all perceive that everyone else is busier than we are, so we protect ourselves from negative judgment by following suit and proclaiming we are also "so busy."

After interviewing a source about the time she spent living in Spain, Schulte was struck by how vastly different the experience of leisure was there when compared with the hectic always-on culture of America. As her source described, "I would have the weekends off. It would feel like a million years. At the end of the weekend, I would feel refreshed. And now that I'm back in the States, Saturdays have become filled with running errands. I don't know how to relax here. Choosing leisure and doing something for pure pleasure is almost a revolutionary, radical choice in the US." It takes real effort (and sometimes shocking forces, like a global pandemic) for people and organizations to stop and ask, "Is this how it should be? Could we do this differently? Do I value different things?"

But it can be done.

Organizational Forces Driving Workaholism

How Organizations Work

Organizations can be thought of as living organisms, each with their own personalities and quirks—that is, their own individual culture. The culture is initially established by the founder(s), based on their own values, personality, and ideals. According to Edgar Schein, one of the leading researchers in this field, organizational culture is the shared values, beliefs, and assumptions held by an organization's members that are the DNA of the company.[15] This means culture is embedded into the organizational structure, procedures, and informal practices.

To establish the culture of their organization, the founder appoints individuals with a similar mindset and vision as them to key leadership positions; company mission statements will reflect the beliefs, values, and assumptions of the founder; and new employees will be selected based on alignment with these values and goals. Over time, the culture becomes further established and reinforced through what industrial-organizational psychologist Ben Schneider calls the ASA model of *attraction, selection,* and *attrition*.[16] Individuals are *attracted* to organizations that embody the same values as they hold. For example, someone that highly values giving back to the community is more likely to be attracted to nonprofits or organizations in helping professions. Someone who is hard-driving and competitive is likely to be attracted to organizations that embrace the #hustle mentality. Similarly, in the *selection* process, hiring managers seek job candidates that possess the key knowledge, skills, abilities, and other characteristics (what we in industrial-organizational psychology call KSAOs) that align with the company's vision and mission. And finally, through the process of *attrition*, individuals who do not fit with the culture of the organization eventually leave.

Think about your decision-making process when you have applied for jobs. I'm sure one of the factors you considered was whether you would be a good fit with the organization, or whether the organization aligned with your core values. What were the things you used to get answers to these questions? Perhaps it was a question to a recruiter or employee about what the average day looked like or what it takes to be successful in the organization. There are many ways to get a feel for an organization's culture, even as an outsider (although you never truly know the culture until you are in it). In short, as sociologist Melissa Mazmanian said to me, "people become their environments to some degree."

But while every organizational culture is unique, the vast majority embrace the work devotion schema, the values that have become ingrained in our capitalist society. So the notions of the ideal worker, and what gets rewarded and punished in this schema, are mirrored within organizations.

Rewarding Overwork

Part of that schema are values that enable workaholism, like placing positive value on overwork. Organizations with an overwork culture operate under a shared assumption that those who are the most devoted—who dedicate the most face time and make the most sacrifices for their jobs—are model examples of employees. Ideally, you are available as close to 24-7 as possible, and you minimize competing obligations. (Often, this is accomplished through a partner who inherits all the other demands of parenting, family obligations, household obligations, and so forth.) Overwork means smudging the line between workdays and non-workdays, and work hours and non-work hours. (So powerful is the work devotion schema that it required legislation to make weekends and days off things in the first place.) Often organizations may acknowledge a "hard-driving" culture of "type As"—which is as much as admitting "We encourage workaholics." But it's wrapped in a competitive imperative—that's just what it takes to succeed in the market.

I have no doubt that people believe this. And I'm certain few organizations have the intention of fostering workaholism as a strategy—simply using up people until they burn out. (It doesn't really work anyway, as I noted in chapter 3. Workaholics are less effective and less productive over the long haul.)

But that's the tricky part of the work devotion schema. It's absorbed so subtly and slowly throughout our lives that it becomes entrenched as an unquestioned reality. When someone says, "We have to do it this way," they mean it, because it would be as hard for them to imagine any other schema as it is hard for us to imagine, say, a world without the color blue. It's just something that exists.

That makes sense when you think about it. How could organizations operate in an ASA model if people thought there was another context besides work devotion? You couldn't attract people if they thought there were options that didn't require devotion, and attrition would be very high because people would see alternatives to work devotion in other organizations.

Organizational Signals

Few companies will deliberately show their level of enabling workaholism, but all organizations give off signals. I refer to these cues as *culture signals*. It's these culture signals that attract individuals to organizations or hint they should stay far away. (Or if you're in the organization—say, in HR—they're the signals of how much an enabler you may be.) It's also the culture signals that let newcomers know what it's *really like* to work there and what they need to do to be successful. Culture signals are often picked up from an intuitive sense after examining many organizations. My first "real" job out of college was as a sales representative for a small print company. I spent a good amount of time walking into businesses all around San Diego, cold-calling or visiting clients. Little did I know, but this job provided me a wonderful opportunity to view a vast array of company cultures and get a feel for the signals they sent off. Each company has its own unique look and feel. I remember the laid-back yet daredevil vibes I got when visiting No Fear's headquarters in Carlsbad, California, with its indoor skateboard ramps, dog park for employees' pets, and full bar at the center of the open-concept office space. Other clients had a more secretive and formal vibe, where employees' desks were tucked away behind closed doors and employees, when they were spotted, were dressed impeccably in professional attire.

But most of you haven't had the opportunities I have had to observe organizational cultures, and in any case, some of those signals won't be reliable. Just because you have a skate park in your office doesn't mean you're not enabling workaholism.

I'll use the ubiquitous iceberg metaphor to describe cultural signals that emanate from organizations. Culture exists at various levels of observability.[17] Only the tip of the culture is visible. The tip of the iceberg that we can see as outsiders of an organization would represent the *organizational artifacts*. Going a bit under the surface, we find the espoused beliefs and values of organizational members. This includes the ideals, goals, values, aspirations, ideologies, and rationalizations. And finally, the deepest down, are the basic underlying assumptions of an organization—the taken-for-granted beliefs and values. These artifacts are laid out in table 4-1.

TABLE 4-1

Examples of specific signals of workaholic culture within an organization

Organizational artifacts	Signs of an overwork/workaholic culture
Physical artifacts	Workaholic jargon is prominently displayed. (*"Thank God It's Monday!"*)
Socialization	Newcomers learn they should be the first in and last out. If you need to leave the office, do so discreetly. (Leave important things at your desk so people assume your break is short.)
Stories and legends	What do people say about the organizational rock stars? What qualities do they highlight (e.g., the long hours put in)?
Norms	Is it typical to work through lunch? Do people talk about or handle family issues while at work? Is there backlash or judgment when someone takes a vacation? What are the communication norms? (Is it common to reach out to people after hours?)
Rituals	Are there mandatory company meetings/retreats during off-work times?
Rewards	Who gets promoted and why? What overwork behaviors are tolerated (and even celebrated) in your organization?
Role models	Do the leaders model workaholic behaviors?

Let's first focus on that visible part of the iceberg, while recognizing they are only telling part of the story. Here are some examples of how the artifacts can help inform our understanding of an organization's overwork culture.

Physical Artifacts

You can learn a lot by looking at the defining features of an organization's building itself or the office space. What is displayed on the walls? For example, software developer Menlo Innovations utilizes shared workspaces, where pairs of developers share a keyboard and monitor—a symbol of the company's value around teamwork.[18] Contrast this with the workspaces of companies such as Theranos, where different departments were separated by locked doors and secrecy was enforced. Think of the different impressions that you get when you walk into an office space adorned with lavish closed-door offices and pictures of the founders adorning the walls compared with many of the Silicon Valley tech companies where offices are replaced with walking desks or common spaces that are filled with foosball tables and beanbag chairs. Do these artifacts signal that the company values tradition? Money? Creativity and innovation?

When looking for signals of an overwork culture, a particular type of artifact I pay attention to are the words, phrases, and company jargon displayed around the office. What does it celebrate? Accomplishments or devotion? Does it praise or implore? Is it inspirational or imposing? Classic examples of this kind of artifact suggesting an overwork culture include the "90 Hours a Week and Loving It!" sweatshirts worn by Macintosh (now Apple) software engineers in the 1980s.[19] Former CEO of Goldman Sachs Hank Paulson reportedly had a sign on his desk that stated, "If you aren't in on Saturday, don't bother showing up on Sunday."[20] Pro football coach Tom Coughlin made waves when he fined several Giants players for arriving only a couple of minutes *early* to meetings, which has been dubbed "Tom Coughlin" time, where five minutes early is on time and on time is late.[21] The message is that this work is more important than anything you were doing before. More recent examples are words and phrases such as "Hustle" or "Thank God It's Monday" plastered on the walls of WeWork.[22]

Be wary of company jargon that glorifies work and working, even if it is framed in a positive manner. For example, phrases such as "Do what you love"—another favorite of WeWork—although it sounds innocuous enough (I mean, who doesn't want to enjoy their work?) can be used to foster a culture where work is play, and play is work. (Put another way, you could do what you love and have it not be work.) Another of WeWork's favorites, "Work hard, play hard," seems to suggest a recognition that employees need to have fulfilling lives outside of work, which is starkly contrasted with employees' actual experiences at the company, where company parties became mandatory and employees were expected to fully devote themselves to the organization.[23]

Socialization

From the moment employees begin working in an organization, they learn what it is like to *actually* work there. Newcomers are socialized by incumbents on what they should and should not be doing and what the leaders and managers pay attention to. Do they talk about their lives outside of work? How quickly should they respond to a supervisor's email on the weekend? How much vacation time should they use? Right from the get-go, Manisha Thakor, founder of the financial well-being consultancy MoneyZen, could tell her new job as an investment banking analyst meant she would spend many sleepless nights working at a frantic and urgent pace. In her book *MoneyZen*, she recalls how she and the other new employees would be bombarded with piles of urgent work that a manager would dump on their desks at 5 p.m., which they then would be working on until the wee hours of the next morning.[24] These early experiences set the tone for what would be expected moving forward.

If you are the person entering an organization, finding out about its culture is tricky because it's often not until you're there that you can pick up these signals. It's helpful in the interview process to speak to current employees and try to glean as many things as you can from what they tell you. For example, in addition to asking about opportunities for advancement, try asking questions like, "Thinking about the past few people to get a promotion, what do you think their most valuable traits and qualities are?" Do you get answers that signal overwork culture? *She was always putting in long hours. They were totally devoted to the company. He was always willing to jump in and help after hours, no matter what he was doing.* During your interviews, take note of whether you are provided with opportunities to have candid conversations with the organization's current employees, or if supervisors or HR reps are always in the room. If the latter, this may signal tight control over the messaging that is being given to recruits; in that case you may get more honest and accurate responses with follow-up one-on-one conversations you can initiate after you have your offer in hand.

For organizations, it's helpful to learn what the socialization of new workers looks like. You may pick up on signals you didn't know existed in your organization. For example, Manisha Thakor recalls a time when she was relatively new in her position and a coworker gave her a tip that if she ever needed to leave the office to take care of a personal matter, she should only take her keys with her. The rationale? If anyone sees her jacket draped over her chair and purse sitting by her desk, they will assume she only briefly stepped away. It makes sense—no one leaves the office without their purse, right? Note that not only does this signal a value for long work hours, but it signals prioritization of being in the office, working, over everything else.

Stories and Legends

Stories and legends signal to newcomers what qualities are celebrated in the organization, and which qualities are punished. Over time, stories become legends, and the values embedded in them are self-perpetuating. Sometimes the stories are about the organization's founder or some other pivotal point in the company history. Other times, the stories are about a specific action taken by the organization or a standout employee—someone who is known for doing something particularly amazing or someone who is held up as an example of what not to do.

In his podcast *WorkLife with Adam Grant*, Grant encourages newcomers to gather stories to understand an organization's culture and offers three great questions you can ask current and former employees (again, these are best asked after you get the offer): (1) "Tell me about something that happens here that wouldn't happen elsewhere," (2) "Tell me about a time when people didn't walk the talk here," and (3) "Tell me a story about who gets hired, promoted, and fired around here."[25] By asking these questions and being a good detective, you can learn a lot about a culture, even from the outside.

Stories can perpetuate and encourage an overwork culture, such as the former professional football coach who was lauded for sleeping in his office for weeks on end and waking up before dawn to start his twenty-hour grind. Or former Yahoo president and CEO Marissa Mayer, who took two weeks off after giving birth to her first child and a few years later took less than a month off after having her twin girls.[26]

Mayer provides an excellent, almost cartoonish example of stories and legends enabling workaholism. In an interview about her time as Google's first female engineer, she described how far she pushed herself:

> The other piece that gets overlooked in the Google story is the value of hard work. When reporters write about Google, they write about it as if it was inevitable. The actual experience was more like, "Could you work 130 hours in a week?" The

answer is yes, if you're strategic about when you sleep, when you shower, and how often you go to the bathroom. The nap rooms at Google were there because it was safer to stay in the office than walk to your car at 3 a.m. For my first five years, I did at least one all-nighter a week, except when I was on vacation—and the vacations were few and far between.[27]

Notice several things about this extraordinary, spectacularly wrongheaded quote creating a legend around Mayer and her employer:

- It suggests that the number of hours of work is directly correlative for organizational success.

- It subtly suggests that if you don't adopt this work ethic, you won't be as successful as her or Google.

- It suggests that you should plan your personal care and well-being around your work, that sleep is subject to the job, and that personal hygiene such as bowel movements should be subservient to your work schedule.

- It celebrates workaholic physical artifacts like nap rooms, which are literally a structural way to keep people connected to work at non-work times.

- It mentions 3 a.m. to signal an organizational norm (more on these in a minute) of working into the middle of the night.

- It suggests all-nighters and forgoing vacation as paths to success.

This is an extreme example, but listen for similar—albeit probably not as strong—signals in your organization or one you're thinking of joining. "Did you hear about the time Randy spent two straight weekends living in his office? He didn't step out of the building a single time. He slept on an air mattress, took showers in the workout room, and ordered Uber Eats and just worked nonstop to meet a deadline." Or "Did you hear about Colleen, who worked straight through the company's holiday party to finish her annual reports?"

The truth within these stories and legends matters far less than their perpetuation. Legends are, by definition, unverified, and usually embellished. It's the fact they're celebrated that matters. That's the signal the culture enables workaholics.

Norms

Each organization has its own unique set of norms, which many times may be different than what is specified in the formal company policies. New employees very quickly learn organizational norms by observation and conversation. What is the typical dress code? Are decisions made collaboratively or only by higher-ups? Who speaks at meetings, and how? Do lower-level employees have autonomy to make decisions on their own, or do they need to be run by the higher-ups first? Do meetings start on time or do they tend to start ten or fifteen minutes late? What's the level of formality between management and employees? All of these are examples of norms that help establish what behavior is expected and what behavior would be seen as unusual. Research has consistently demonstrated the powerful effects of organizational norms on employee work behaviors.[28]

There are many examples of organizational norms that may unintentionally or intentionally encourage an overwork culture. Do coworkers typically have lunch together or work through lunch at their desks? If it's common to work through lunch, this signals that it's more important to not interrupt work than it is for employees to take a break or socialize with each other. What time do people typically get to work and what time do they leave? Do they work on weekends or answer work calls in the evening? Is it typical for employees to handle a family issue while at work, or is this frowned upon? How quickly are decisions made and action taken—is there a high level of urgency or is work done more slowly and consistently? Are employees allowed to work from home? At Yahoo, Marissa Mayer banned work from home when she arrived, setting a clear norm that signaled to workers that presence in an office was more important than flexibility. The pandemic served as a real-time referendum on such policies that is still playing out to this day. Companies mandating return to work are signaling that they are workaholic enablers, but they're now facing a more competitive market for talent with other companies that discovered through necessity that mandatory office time was wildly overrated as a driver of productivity by many companies. Still, many can't accept the data that shows little effect on productivity from more flexible work schedules. The work devotion schema is hard to quit.

Social psychology has shown for decades that when people deviate from norms, they may be "punished" in a variety of ways. A classic example in our field comes from the Hawthorne studies—a series of social experiments that went on for a decade in Western Electric's Hawthorne Works plant. The studies are best known for the discovery of the famous *Hawthorne effect* that showed bumps in productivity when the workers who were the focus of the experiments knew they were being observed, but another, lesser-known set of experiments in the plant involved observations of a group of workers in the bank wiring department (who installed "banks" of electrical wiring into rooms).[29] In this department, employees had a preferred work pace that they ensured new employees fell in line with—about 1.5 banks per day—and were paid a daily wage. When management offered to move to a piece-rate pay system, so that if they installed more banks they were paid more, the men resisted, fearing that the company would use the piece-rate system until the workers showed that they could do three banks per day, and then would revert to the daily wage, with increased expectations of productivity. Thus, the bank wiring employees prevented others from disrupting what they felt was a fair day's work for a fair day's pay. When an overzealous and eager employee started working at a faster pace than was the norm, the new employee received a "bing"—a whack on the arm with the middle knuckle extended a bit so it could really hurt a muscle—until they slowed down their pace to be in line with the group.[30] Another example that indicates overwork culture is the norm in which everyone works until later into the evening, but you leave at 7 p.m. and your coworker quips, "Half day, eh?"

In their book *Why Work Sucks and How to Fix It*, Cali Ressler and Jody Thompson call this pushback *sludge*. Sludge, according to Ressler and Thompson, is any negative comment that serves to reinforce old ideas about how work gets done; that is, the status quo. An example they provide is someone saying, "*Another* vacation? How many vacation days do you get? I haven't taken a vacation in five years!" because they can't say what they are *really* thinking: "You're a slacker. Only people who sacrifice their time are committed to their jobs."[31]

In many cases, 24-7 devotion to the company is reinforced by expectations that employees will attend all expected-but-not-required activities. Oh, that company outing on the first Saturday of each month? Yeah, that is *technically* optional, but no one wants to face the boss on Monday if they skip it, as the boss makes it very clear he isn't happy about it. You had plans with your kids? You could have just brought them with you (meaning—family needs to fit into your work, not the other way around).

Connectivity and communication norms are critically important signals to evaluate. Overwork culture is reinforced when there
is pressure to be always on, to respond immediately to work calls,
texts, and emails. What is the shared understanding of the need
to be connected or reachable to one another? Are supervisors constantly texting or calling employees outside of traditional work
hours? Are employees expected to respond immediately to these
messages, and what happens if they don't? Does your organization
use an app such as Slack or Teams that encourages 24-7 communication? What happens when a team member silences notifications
on their phone? I'm not just talking about pressure to respond
to coworkers or your boss, by the way. Pressure to immediately
respond to customers can be just as powerful in shaping beliefs
that you must be constantly available to your work.

It's not just about these communication patterns, though. It's
also about the content of the communication. Do employees ever
talk about important life events, such as a child's birthday, a wedding anniversary, or an upcoming family vacation? Or is the conversation all about who had the highest sales figures that month or
how to meet this month's goals? When time off is used or someone
leaves work early, do people casually say, "Hey, I'm taking off at 3
to catch my daughter's soccer game" or do they slide out the back
door in secrecy?

What are the norms around taking time off? Some organizations will crow about how much vacation they offer as a sign they
are not enabling workaholism. Some have even adopted unlimited
vacation days as a perk. But a more important signal is how much
vacation time is *used*. Just because an organization offers unlimited vacation days doesn't mean its employees feel safe taking those
days. A company that touts unlimited vacation days may simply
be masking its workaholic culture. This is one of those examples

of a mismatch between espoused company values and its true cultural DNA.

Rituals

Like norms, rituals can be formal or informal. A yearly offsite is a ritual. Who's invited? What are the themes? Who presents and who listens? What other group activities are repeated over time? What accomplishments are celebrated in the organization? WeWork's mandatory "Thank God It's Monday!" meeting (held at 7 p.m.) celebrating the start of a new workweek is a prime example of a ritual signaling work devotion.[32]

Informal rituals can also signal if a culture is actively or passively enabling workaholism. Do sales teams have status competitions for who books the most hotel stays that year or who has flown the most miles with their favorite airline?

Rewards

When employees earn accolades and awards, what are they for? What the company's leaders pay attention to, reward, and talk about focuses their followers' attention and drives efforts in that direction.[33] As Adam Grant says, "The most direct way to figure out what's valued in a culture isn't to listen to what people say is important. It's to pay attention to who gets rewarded and promoted to leadership roles. Groups elevate people who represent their principles and advance their goals."[34]

And as I said at the close of chapter 2, our research shows workaholics often end up getting promoted to managerial levels. Those rewards alone signal a culture that enables overwork.

What other qualities are highly prized in your organization? In an organization with a workaholic culture, a "Put work first" mentality is implicitly or explicitly rewarded. Who are the star employees in the organization, and what makes them stand out? Are they rewarded for their performance or their performative workaholism?[35] Are they consistently the first ones in the office or the last ones to leave? Do they constantly put their jobs ahead of their families or personal lives? If these behaviors are rewarded, it signals to employees that success requires you to prioritize work over everything else.

Some organizations don't hide what they are rewarding. One summer in college, I had a grueling job selling books door-to-door from 7:30 in the morning until 8:00 in the evening, Monday through Saturday. For three months straight, I worked my butt off in this job—which, it turned out, I was really great at. I received an award for the hours I was putting in, called the Gold Seal Award, and it came with a commemorative coin. On the front of the coin, it listed our accomplishments: thirty sales presentations each day, seventy-five hours worked per week. On the back, four words: Integrity, Goals, Competition, and Trainable. Looking back on this time in my life, I realized not only was the company explicitly rewarding overwork (along with the Gold Seal Award, I also won a trip to Jamaica for my high sales numbers), but that I was rationalizing why it was such a great thing that I just spent my summer working eighty-plus hours per week—*Look at all the money I made! I'm in the best shape of my life!*

Beyond what is explicitly rewarded, overwork signals can be sent simply by *tolerating* certain behaviors. Steve Gruenert and Todd Whitaker point this out in their book *School Culture Rewired*, stating, "The culture of any organization is shaped by the worst behavior the leader is willing to tolerate."[36] So, Eve is working on Fridays, even though your work team decided to take every other Friday off? If the supervisor lets this slide, this can signal that even though you have a new rule in place, it's meant to be broken.

Role Models

When we see workaholic behaviors modeled by those we look up to, we begin to mimic them. Psychologist Albert Bandura wrote about the concept of observational learning in his theory of social learning.[37] Anyone who has taken a psychology class has probably heard of Bandura's classic "Bobo doll" experiments, where children observed an adult role model playing with toys and were then allowed to play with the toys themselves. His research showed children who observed an adult playing aggressively with an inflatable Bobo doll were far more likely to also play aggressively with the doll compared with children who observed adults playing in a non-aggressive manner.

"OK," you may be thinking. "Sure—but that experiment was conducted on children. Are you really trying to argue that as adults, we are that influenced by the behaviors of others around us?" No, of course not. But I am arguing that we are absolutely shaped by the environments around us.

Why is this?

Although we may not model behavior of others in the simplistic way the children did in Bandura's experiment, we do pay attention to others around us to judge what is acceptable and unacceptable. As children, we learn by watching what our parents do and we emulate them. And as adults, we learn what is desired and expected by the organization by watching our mentors and role models at work. We also pay attention to what behaviors are rewarded. Let me go back to the communication norms to give an example of how behavior of a supervisor can signal what is expected of employees. Professor Melissa Mazmanian conducted an experiment examining smartphone use in organizations. She found that when supervisors always responded promptly to text messages, subordinates would subsequently feel strong pressure to also respond quickly to messages on their phones.[38] Researcher Yue Lok Cheung found that workaholics were particularly sensitive to these types of cues about pressure to use smartphones after work, which in turn led to them using smartphones more often.[39]

Leaders generally don't understand what effect their small behaviors have on their organizations and its culture. Often, it's not malicious, and if you confronted a leader, they might say, "Well I don't expect a reply right away, even if I reply instantly. That's just me." But it doesn't matter. Implicitly, the message is received by others to emulate the behavior.

Taking Stock

Hopefully, as you read this chapter, you are thinking about the signals in your own organization. Whether you're an individual worried about how your organization may be enabling your workaholic tendencies, or close to someone whom you're concerned about, it helps to seek out these signals to mitigate workaholism and its enablers. If you're someone who's in charge of an organization or its policies, such as in HR, doing so may be revealing uncomfortable truths about the culture of your organization.

Now take a minute and think of your company's artifacts. Do any of them implicitly or explicitly endorse a workaholic culture? What are you doing to enable an overwork culture? Table 4-2 is a template version of table 4-1 that allows you to take notes regarding organizational artifacts that may be specific signals of workaholic culture within your organization. Writing them out can help you see patterns and start to know where to target the enablers.

And remember, don't be fooled by what your organization *says* it values. You should write down what actually happens. Just as

TABLE 4-2

Template for finding specific signals of workaholic culture within your organization

Organizational artifacts	Signs of an overwork/workaholic culture
Physical artifacts	
Socialization	
Stories and legends	
Norms	
Rituals	
Rewards	
Role models	

with the individual exercises in previous chapters, this exercise requires you to be open and honest. You need to force yourself to take a hard, critical look at reality, not the reality you espouse. Just as with vacation time offered versus taken, the salient point to note in the table isn't that the company's value statement touts the importance of work-life balance. It's that Trent got a promotion and it was noted that he works harder and longer than anyone in the promotion notice. You might discover that some of your espoused values are the butt of jokes and memes among employees. That's what you're after when uncovering the enabling factors.

Classic examples of a mismatch between espoused values and actual values are companies like Enron. The culture at Enron was ripe with secrecy and deceit. Yet their stated corporate values were communication, respect, integrity, and excellence.[40] WeWork comes up again and again because it's such a clear example of a mismatch between what it said it was and what it actually was. WeWork emphasized the importance of authenticity, yet put tracking bracelets on its employees to ensure they attended mandatory meetings at its annual summer camp—a seventy-two-hour weekend rager filled with seminars and lots of booze. It embraced the phrase "Work hard, play hard," while at the same time cofounder and CEO Adam Neumann preached to his employees to "work until you drop."[41] And as Brigid Schulte pointed out to me, don't focus on whether your organization touts its wellness programs, mindfulness coach, and lunchtime yoga. Focus instead on whether you get emails from your boss at ten o'clock each night. By saying one thing but doing another, Schulte says, you can create more cynicism and more skepticism.

Strong cultures make it harder to deviate from what is assumed to be the "right" way to work—the "way we do things around here." They also are more likely to foster devout loyalty to the organization. However, as pointed out by researchers Anne Schaef and Diane Fassel in their book *The Addictive Organization*, "When loyalty to the organization becomes a substitute for living one's own life, then the company has become the addictive substance of choice. . . . The issue is not benefits per se, but the way the organization and individuals use them to stay central in the lives of workers and consequently to prevent people from moving on and doing what they need to do."[42]

Beginning to Change

Organizations with strong cultures tend to be more stubborn when it comes to change. And in a capitalist economy, it's hard to ratchet down an overwork culture, particularly in a publicly held organization where shareholders are concerned about maximizing profits and increasing stock prices. Your organization had a good year this year? Great! How can we make it even better next year? Success only brings the desire for more success.

Recognizing the signals of an overwork culture is a start. You can't alter culture until you've documented what it really is (not what you tell the world it is). That starts the hard work of change, but then there's more to do, and I'll discuss in both chapter 5 and the conclusion the kinds of interventions that can begin to target your own workaholism and a company's culture of workaholism.

For the entrepreneurs and self-employed individuals who are reading this chapter and thinking, *OK, but this is not relevant for me because I am the one making all of these decisions*, it may be helpful to reflect on what signals you may be sending to *yourself.*

Many of the individuals I spoke with are business owners, entrepreneurs, and self-employed professionals. Veronica, a self-employed psychotherapist in private practice, was not beholden to anyone besides herself. She recalls that she was seeing forty patients a week within the first year of opening her private practice internship. She couldn't turn people away. It wasn't until her health started declining that she finally decided to address her self-imposed overwork culture. With the help of her mentor, Veronica finally managed to make changes to her workaholic behavior. She raised her rates and closed her practice on Saturdays. To reinforce her newly revamped practice, Veronica placed an index card on her desk where it was always visible. The card contained a slogan she had gotten from Workaholics Anonymous: "My life is full and underscheduled. I say no, even when offered the best." This was Veronica's new mantra, and she'd repeat it out loud when she found herself feeling pressure to work more.

Still, having a mantra and following through on it aren't the same. No matter if the workaholic culture is imposed by the organization or yourself, changing is difficult. The temptations are always there to go back to the way things were, Veronica told me. "Prospective clients would call and say, 'So-and-so told me you're a great therapist; I am only looking to see you.' Having to say, 'I'm sorry, my practice is full' were the hardest words I've ever spoken in my life." Over time, though, Veronica did continue to follow this mantra, and she eventually reduced her schedule to around fourteen patients a week, working Monday through Wednesday.

Changing a culture is not as simple as changing some of the organization's artifacts, as these efforts will only work for so long since they don't really address the cultural DNA of the organization. Culture is deep and, as such, difficult to change without concerted effort. Edgar Schein has a metaphor of a lily pond to represent the culture of an organization.[43] Imagine a lily pond with blossoms and leaves floating on the surface of the pond—these visible features represent the artifacts. Underneath the water are the seeds and roots representing the espoused values and beliefs, which are nourished by the quality of the water in the pond (the underlying assumptions) and the fertilizers used by the farmer (the company's founder).

To change the lily pond so that a different color blossoms is not as simple as painting the blossoms a different color. This only lasts until the color wears off or the blossoms die, and then the initial color reemerges. Instead, the change must begin by changing the invisible features of the pond—the cultural DNA. How can the seeds, the quality of the water, the fertilizer used be changed? Only by changing these factors can the pond begin to evolve, and the change be sustained over time.

Key Takeaways

- Overwork culture is embedded into a variety of practices and norms within the organization.

- The organization is situated in a societal context that also encourages and reinforces overwork.

- Pay attention to organizational signals that enable workaholism: physical artifacts, socialization, stories and legends, company norms, rituals, who is rewarded, and whether leaders and stars exhibit workaholic behaviors.

- Take note of mismatches between what the organization *says* it values and what it *actually* values.

- Surface-level organizational changes will not make a long-lasting impact. Focus on the deeper cultural DNA.

CHAPTER 5

Fixing Your Culture of Overwork

"That's a great idea in theory, but that won't work here."
"Our customers demand we are available 24-7."
"High performers can manage the work."

When talking to organizations about workaholism—and how they may be enabling it—I've heard every excuse you can imagine, multiple times. In an organization with an overwork culture, it's natural and not all that surprising. For one, the company has succeeded using this approach. Why change it? For another, what I'm suggesting is that it doesn't work as well as one might think, and the organization ought to change. Given everything we know about organizational culture and how difficult it is to change it, resistance is natural—expected even.

And just as I said about individuals at the end of chapter 3, for organizations, escaping their overwork culture that enables workaholics takes practice and discipline. It's hard stuff. Organizations may make some progress but then slide back into old, familiar patterns that allow for or even encourage overwork. This is why culture change is so hard. Not only is the overwork culture embedded into a variety of practices and norms within the organization, the organization is situated in a societal context that also encourages and reinforces overwork, as we learned last chapter.

Like individuals, organizations are typically not going to willingly seek to change their overwork culture until some event or situation serves as a wake-up call. Perhaps the company was faced with the reality of an employee dying as a direct result of its overwork culture. Maybe the CEO suffers a major health scare caused by overwork and has a sudden desire to revamp the corporate culture. Maybe a revolt by key employees leaves a massive talent hole in the organization. Maybe the Covid-19 pandemic opened up the top echelon in the organization to taking employee health (physical and mental) more seriously.

I've worked with enough organizations to know that most will continue to maintain their overwork culture until they are faced with something that truly makes them question it.

In August 2013, Moritz Erhardt, a Bank of America Merrill Lynch intern in London, was found dead in his shower of an epileptic seizure, having worked seventy-two hours straight.[1] Responding to his death, the bank launched a global review of working hours and curtailed the number of days in a row an intern could work.

And thirty-one-year-old Japanese journalist Miwa Sado died from heart failure attributed to overwork after logging 159 hours of overtime in one month. Let's put that in perspective. There are 744 hours in a thirty-one-day month. Assuming a person worked 10 hours per day before overtime, and assuming they slept 6 hours a night, someone who adds 159 hours of overtime to that schedule has about 89 hours of non-work and non-sleep time. That leaves only 3 hours per day for *all other* activities in one's life: eating, shopping, commuting, laundry, and anything else.

Sado's death, along with the death of twenty-four-year-old Matsuri Takahashi the previous year—also linked to overwork—prompted calls to limit overtime and put pressure on Japanese prime minister Shinzo Abe to address systemic cultural problems relating to overwork culture.[2] Data from the Ministry of Health, Labour, and Welfare shows a steady increase in claims relating to *karoshi* (death from overwork) and *karojisatsu* (death by suicide induced by overwork). According to this data, between 2015 and 2019, the number of claims relating to *karoshi* and *karojisatsu* total almost thirteen thousand.[3]

In one of the most comprehensive studies of the negative effects of overwork, the World Health Organization (WHO) and International Labour Organization compiled data from over 194 countries from 2000 to 2016. Their study found 745,000 deaths from stroke and ischemic heart disease that could be linked to long working hours, an increase of 28 percent since 2000.[4] Notably, many of those who died weren't currently working long hours, but they had done so at an earlier point in their career. In her book *MoneyZen*, Manisha Thakor makes the comparison to the negative health effects of smoking. Smoking may not kill you immediately, but that doesn't mean it won't negatively affect your health down the road. So, even if you quit overworking now, it can still lead to early death later.[5]

Even if they haven't faced such dire consequences, virtually everyone I've spoken with about their workaholism experienced extreme burnout, which is obviously bad for organizations. Recently, the WHO updated its definition of burnout to clarify that it is an *occupational* phenomenon linked to chronic workplace stress.[6] Employee burnout is extremely costly to organizations—some peg this amount at up to $300 billon a year.[7]

Or perhaps the issue facing your organization is high turnover. According to the Society for Human Resource Management, it costs organizations about a third of a worker's annual earnings to replace them if they leave.[8] If your organization is churning through employees, overworking them out of the job, there are direct costs to your organization from that culture.

The problem of overwork culture was so bad at Goldman Sachs that a group of junior bankers created and circulated an informal survey to their coworkers to document what they described as abusive working conditions. In the survey, the analysts said they worked almost hundred-hour weeks and slept only five hours per week on average.[9] According to one analyst, they were working so much that they were not eating, showering, or doing anything else from morning until after midnight. Analysts also reported a marked decline in their mental and physical health, dropping to 2.8 and 2.1, respectively, compared with 8.8 and 9.0 from before starting at Goldman (ratings were on a scale ranging from 1 to 10, with 10 being healthiest). Some bankers reported working eighteen-hour shifts, and one London-based banker reported that at any time there were between three to six bankers per team on sick leave due to burnout.[10] After the report circulated on social media, Goldman vowed to address the employee complaints. However, a year after these issues were brought to light, news articles reported that little appeared to have changed.[11]

Overcoming Pushback: The Evidence Doesn't Lie

If you don't want to be one of these organizations, something needs to change. And despite the default responses you have about why change won't work for you or how your people can sustain the pace, it's not true—and the alternative to your current modus operandi is not as bad as you think.

The pushback to changing a workaholic culture is similar to the pushback that companies gave for why remote work wouldn't work prior to the pandemic. But when Covid happened and organizations had no choice, they realized overwhelmingly that their assumptions about remote work were unfounded and even counter to reality. In many places, productivity rose. Conservative industries like banking were shocked to see positive results.

Still not convinced? Then check out the breakthrough findings about the indisputable success of the four-day workweek movement.[12] The idea of a four-day workweek is not new. In her book *The Overworked American*, Juliet Schor notes that by the late 1950s, experts were predicting the four-day week would "loom on the immediate horizon."[13] Fifty years ago, scholars argued that the most serious barrier to widespread adoption of the four-day week would be the attitudes of upper management.[14] It seems not much has changed.

I asked Andrew Barnes, cofounder of not-for-profit coalition 4 Day Week Global, what inspired him to start implementing these trials at his own company, Perpetual Guardian. He recalled to me what work was like for him in his twenties in the banking industry in London. His employer at the time opened before the Tokyo markets closed and stayed open until US trading was done, which meant his working day was structured to be twelve-plus hours. In addition to that, there was travel time to and from London—for him an hour-and-a-half train ride each way. If he missed the 7:30 train at night, which he often did, the next train wasn't until 9:30, meaning he wouldn't get home until 11 p.m.

There was a tremendous amount of performance pressure at that job, Barnes recalled. He witnessed two people having nervous breakdowns in front of him, including his boss. Realizing this was unsustainable not just for him but for his own team, he began to think of how his management style impacted others' overwork and paid more attention to how overwork was impacting those around him.

At the national level, four-day workweek trials have been happening for more than a decade across several countries in the Nordic region, including Iceland, Sweden, and Finland.[15] Encouraged by the positive outcomes of these initial trials, 4 Day Week Global launched the world's largest trial to date.[16] A total of sixty-one companies so far across the United States, United Kingdom, Australia, New Zealand, and Canada have participated in the trial. To participate, companies had to agree to a reduction in employees' work time with no reduction in pay. Most of the companies restructured their workweek around a four-day, thirty-two-hour-per-week schedule. The trial consisted of two months of preparation and onboarding for each company followed by a six-month trial period. Surveys were distributed throughout the trial period to capture employee well-being and performance outcomes, and interviews were conducted with the company's key leaders and employees before, during, and after the trial. Other important metrics such as revenue, absenteeism, new hires, and resignations were also gathered.

Here are some key highlights of the most recent trial.[17]

- Employee well-being dramatically improved. At the end of the trial, 39 percent of employees were less stressed and 71 percent had reduced levels of burnout than before the trial. Mental and physical health improved, while anxiety, fatigue, and sleep issues decreased.

- Employees reported improved work-life balance and greater satisfaction with household finances, relationships, how their time was managed, and overall life satisfaction.

- Eighty-one percent of employees perceived either no changes or increases in their current work ability compared to their lifetime best.

- Ninety-two percent of companies indicated they plan on continuing the four-day workweek after trial.

- Company revenue rose by 1.4 percent on average over the six-month trial period.

- Comparing company revenue to a similar period from previous years, organizations reported an average 35 percent increase.

And finally, two striking data points:

- This trial took place in the middle of the Great Resignation, when millions of workers were voluntarily quitting their jobs. Despite this, employee turnover at these companies dropped by 57 percent over the trial period.[18]

- When asked whether they would want to continue with the four-day workweek after the trial period, 96 percent indicated they would like to continue (90 percent of these responded with the most enthusiastic option of "Yes/Definitely"). Moreover, 15 percent of employees indicated that *no amount of money* would entice them to accept a five-day schedule moving forward.

The four-day week initiative is not the only shining example of successful organizational change. There is also the organizational change initiative called STAR (Support. Transform. Achieve. Results.), which was developed and implemented by the Work, Family, and Health Network, a large research team of psychologists,

sociologists, economists, public health, and family scholars supported by the National Institutes of Health and the Centers for
Disease Control and Prevention. The STAR program operates
through a dual-agenda work redesign that seeks to address (1) organizational concerns (working effectively) and (2) employee concerns
(working in ways that are sustainable).[19] What I like about STAR
is that it challenges the 24-7, always-on culture norm—and other
previously taken-for-granted assumptions about what it means to
be a high-performing employee—head-on.

The data is overwhelming and indisputable. The fact it has
taken so long to get here speaks to just how difficult and scary
change can be, and how deeply the inertia of organizational
norms and the work devotion scheme root themselves in our
lives. Resistance to the reduction of work time and a shift away
from overwork norms should erode in the face of such evidence.
(There is evidence from previous examples, too. When factory
owners began to limit workdays to ten, and then eight, hours
in response to organized labor demands, management was surprised to discover that output increased while expensive mistakes and accidents decreased.[20]) And I suspect it will, but it will
take time.

In the meantime, there are steps you can take as an organization to overcome the resistance and institute change.[21] Regardless of the reason for the desire to change, simply having that
desire is a great step in the right direction. Reading this book is
an excellent step, too. It helps you understand the mechanisms
that drive individuals' workaholic tendencies and some of the
interventions that individuals can take (and you can provide,
as a forward-looking organization that wants to take care of its
employees).

Disassembling a Culture of Overwork

Once you've acknowledged that change is needed, you'll need to create a plan for how you'll overcome a culture of workaholism. Below is a three-step process to start.

Step 1: Assess Your Company's Baseline
Level of Overwork and Its Origins

Figure out where your starting point is by assessing the level of your organization's overwork culture and who is perpetuating it. What you do next will depend on where your baseline is.

Borrowing a concept from training and organizational change literatures, I recommend starting with a needs assessment. This helps to identify areas in need of change, assesses how much support (or resistance) there is to the change initiative, and allows for a comprehensive understanding of training needs at multiple levels of analysis.[22]

There are many frameworks for needs assessments you could adopt. In general, they attempt to answer two key questions:

- What are the areas in need of change?

- What kind of support is there for making this change happen?

The assessment should be handled by people with experience doing them—for example, professionals who have been trained in change management. Relationships with top-level managers in the organization need to be established. Some of these managers will react with fear or resistance. Anyone who is an *Office Space* fan will remember the fear and skepticism that employees had toward

"The Bobs" (clueless efficiency consultants, for those of you who are not familiar with the movie)—and you definitely will want to avoid that. People who do needs or change assessments regularly know how to read the reactions they get and what they mean in terms of commitment to change.

They're also good at establishing the necessary psychological safety that large change initiatives demand and then putting structures in place to ensure anonymity that will allow the frank discussions that need to take place to assess the workplace. If people feel threatened by the change and aren't reassured that they are protected from retribution, the initiative is destined to fail.

The overwork culture assessment should target three levels:

- Organizational level: What is driving the culture of overwork?

- Job level: How is the structure of jobs driving workaholism?

- Personal level: What are the characteristics of individuals who get recognized and rewarded, and do those qualities reinforce an overwork culture? How do people feel about their work and the company?

At the organizational level, much time will be spent with cultural factors, such as the underlying values and assumptions about working at the organization. It will look at declared versus actual values and it will use mined data. Are people taking their allotted vacation? They will also assess if top leadership is unwittingly sending signals that discourage disconnection from work—all the signs I talked about in chapter 4. Culture surveys, interviews, analysis of leadership communication, and even observation of work activity will inform this (preferably all led by trained professionals or researchers who can implement best data collection and survey development practices).

At the job level, the assessment will dig into structures that encourage overwork, including the type of technology used to get jobs done: Does it encourage or even demand 24-7 connection? It will examine workflows: Do some tasks put people in positions of needing to overwork? And it will assess job design: Are jobs built to give individuals too much work? Is staffing lean to a fault? And so forth.

For example, a medical device company I consulted with gathered analytics from productivity tools like email, calendars, and chat programs. Content of the communications wasn't gathered, just the metadata of when and where they happened and how much they happened. Information was also collected on how many meetings were held and how long they were. When were they held? By pairing this with data on workers' stress levels, the company could determine if jobs were structured to demand overwork.

At the personal level, the assessment will zoom in a bit further to examine the individuals within the organization. What are the qualities and characteristics of the individuals who get recognized and rewarded, and do those qualities reinforce an overwork culture? For example, do people who work weekends get promoted? Are those people taking their paid time off (PTO)? Second, identify the key players—both the supporters (champions) of the change initiative as well as the likely derailers. Finally, the personal level assessment also is a time to get a sense of the workforce's attitudes and feelings about their work and the company. What are people saying about their level of energy, stress, or feelings about being disconnected from work?

At the end of the assessment, you'll know just how deeply overwork is entrenched in your culture and, crucially, where some of the key drivers are coming from. In some organizations, it may be almost exclusively driven by leadership. Others may have let technology foster an always-on workforce. Others will focus on job design and HR structures. Surveys and interviews are likely to expose physical and mental health issues and team dysfunctions, driven by workaholism, that you simply weren't aware were present in the organization.

Step 2: Plan for Incremental Change by Targeting Places Where Change Will Be Most Effective Soonest

At this point, the worst thing you could do as an organization is to say, "We're going to get rid of our overwork culture and eliminate workaholism." Change doesn't work that way. It will be a long process of incremental improvements. The key is that the assessment will tell you where to focus first. Where is change going to be both most possible and most effective?

Remember Gabe, who had his "aha!" moment after watching *The Notebook*? After he was able to get hold of his own workaholism, he set his sights on reshaping his company's culture of overwork, which was fueled by his "fear machine" leadership style (described in chapter 3). Today, the mission of his company, G2i, is to promote developer health and well-being by matching developers with companies that offer a four-day workweek. More than just a recruitment platform, G2i also provides resources to organizations seeking to experiment with culture change that challenges overwork culture.

When a company comes to G2i wanting to hire developers, Gabe's team carefully screens them to see whether the company practices what they preach in terms of promoting developer health, or whether it's just overwork culture disguised as a flexible workplace. The team at G2i spends a lot of time educating them on G2i's developer health mission and why this approach will allow them to hire better people. This education-based approach has been so effective that the company has plans to develop additional content to promote their company's purpose—inviting people to live a healthier worklife.

At this stage, the most important things to do are to clearly identify the purpose and goals of the trial, build trust, carefully outline what the trial period will involve, and clearly communicate the plan to all key constituents.

Identify the purpose and goals of the trial. Your purpose will be shaped by the data you have gathered and analyzed as part of your assessment. When examining your organization's baseline levels of overwork culture, it may become clear that pursuing goals such as a four-day workweek is not possible. In these cases, the goal may need to be something smaller—what researchers Leslie Perlow and her team call "micro adjustments to the work practices"—such as changing guidelines around email communication during non-work time or on weekends.[23]

Your organizational and job-level assessments help guide decisions about what the trial experiment will target. Will it involve changes to work hours, or perhaps changes in communication norms and expectations? For example, say your organization sees technology as a prime culprit in its workaholic culture and a place to focus for maximizing change. Change efforts could involve removing email from everyone's phones or imposing email blackouts coupled with a focus on creating new rules about communication times or methods. Another organization may prioritize changes to aspects of its broader company culture, such as the messaging in its physical artifacts and its communication, having realized they were implicitly encouraging workaholism. Their communication may focus on changing their public-space messaging by 80 percent in six months and surveying employees on the effect. Perhaps another recognizes that its reward system is driving people to workaholism and plans to revamp its evaluation criteria for promotions and change some internal communications to celebrate detachment from work.

Your purpose and goals will also be shaped to address the key issues noted by employees in the baseline surveys. Are your goals to address employee burnout and work-family conflict? Or do you want to increase motivation and engagement? If there are specific aspects of the employee experience that you want to target in your intervention, make sure to assess these prior to the trial experiment so you have a baseline assessment to compare any post-intervention surveys to.

Build trust from the ground up, not the top down. Andrew Barnes describes building trust as the "magic bullet" of a successful four-day workweek intervention. It's also something that cannot be forged overnight. Before running his trials at Perpetual Guardian, Barnes had proved to his staff that he was committed to investing in the long-term success of the business and to the people within it. If your organization does not have trust as a key part of its culture, it's probably not ready for this type of culture change. Without this trust, Barnes says, the cynics and detractors will almost certainly derail the best intentions of the supporters and adopters.

Trust can come only if culture change efforts involve input from *all* employees—it cannot come from the top down. In fact, Barnes says the fact that it's an employee-led process is one of the key factors that makes any four-day workweek initiative successful. To help build this trust, John Kotter recommends building a "guiding coalition"—a group of individuals from all levels of the organization who are passionate about the change initiative and are respected by their peers.[24]

It's important to focus trust-building efforts on the potential derailers of your change initiative. These individuals are likely to cause obstacles or roadblocks down the road—or even worse, may be "game-enders."[25] For example, Andrew Barnes also noted that one of the biggest hurdles in his four-day workweek trials was the attitude of management. Even when he mandated that managers take their fifth day off, some would simply work from home on that day in secret, while others took the fifth day off but worked more hours on the other four days (which defeated the purpose).[26] Develop contingency plans for addressing issues caused by potential derailers if trust-building efforts are unsuccessful.

Carefully outline the trial experiment. In my conversations with leaders designing experiments, a couple of things stand out. The first is to resist overthinking to the point that the plan becomes too complex to carry out. Approach the process with an experimental mindset, knowing that you will adapt as you go. Set a concrete start and end date. Identify the scope of the trial—in other words, which team(s) will be involved in the initial trials and how this will be rolled out over time. And be sure to collect pretrial data on anything you'll be assessing at the conclusion of the trial. For example, if your purpose is to decrease employee burnout, then make sure to assess burnout before the employees even catch wind of the trial (so you can conduct more accurate pre-post comparisons). I highly recommend utilizing the help of experts anytime you are gathering employee survey data. Gabe also recommends planning the trial period during a slower time of the year.

Clearly communicate the plan and keep the conversation going. It's not enough to simply tell key stakeholders, *Look, we're going to fix our workaholic culture with a new initiative.* You must communicate specifics of your effort and what you're hoping to accomplish with each experiment. Communication should also not be top down—frequent two-way communication is essential. Seek input from your employees before, during, and after the trial experiment. Make sure you are listening and responding to their concerns. Andrew Barnes, in his book *The 4 Day Week*, emphasizes the importance of continually asking employees for their views, as it presents an opportunity "to take an inclusive role in committing to the initiative and guiding and coaching their teams."[27] Researcher Leslie Perlow and her team called this "structured dialogue"—an ongoing conversation that is a critical part of the success of such a change initiative.[28] Perlow further recommends scheduling regular meetings for structured dialogue where attendance is mandatory. In their pilot at Boston Consulting Group, Perlow's team implemented communication-generating tools to foster dialogues in the meetings, such as pulse checks (where meeting team members were asked a series of structured questions to gauge their feelings and thoughts about the trial experiment) as well as "tummy rumbles," where team members could voice concerns before meetings (for example, maybe a shared document where individuals can post anonymous concerns and questions).

Step 3: Execute the Trial Experiment, Learn, and Iterate

With a plan in place, it's time to execute. Contrary to what you might want to do, you shouldn't announce major changes; you shouldn't even suggest that you've "figured it out."

Start small and meet people where they are. Limit the number of changes you take on and their scope. You may start with one team or department. Or one geography. And make sure you are constantly taking the temperature of employees about the change initiatives. Avoid being ambiguous in your execution. When people aren't certain about what is happening, they will become risk avoidant and fall back into old patterns.

Say one of your change experiments is to require email signatures that say, "Don't feel pressured to respond to this in non-work hours." That seems good, but it remains ambiguous. It doesn't say "Don't respond." And what if it's from a boss? It might be interpreted like one of those "voluntary" get-togethers that people informally know is actually mandatory. Perhaps the experiment shows that people kept responding to emails despite this. The next step may be to change the language to something like "Do not respond after work hours," or to even set up rules that prevent emails from being delivered at certain hours.

. . .

None of these steps will be easy. Edgar Schein points out that culture change involves *unlearning* something as well as learning something.[29] So people must first unlearn the behaviors that reinforce an overwork mentality—ones they may have internalized or even formalized. Then they have to learn new work patterns and behaviors. Even with simple changes this is difficult. Habits are hard to break.

Strategies for Actionable Change

Every organization is different, and the changes yours will make will depend on your baseline and how far your organization is willing (at first!) to go to overcome its culture of overwork. But there are some actionable strategies that you can use to guide your plans. As you begin executing on your effort to change a workaholic-enabling culture, keep these ideas in mind to guide the changes you make.

Reward Output, Not Input

Barnes believes it's the failure to understand how to appropriately measure output that's at the heart of organizations' resistance to change their overwork culture. In a manufacturing economy, it's easier. An employee who produces twenty widgets is more productive than an employee who produces ten. In a service-based economy, we can no longer measure productivity in terms of widgets per hour, so what do we use instead? Our tendency is to use time as a proxy for performance, rewarding employees for the hours put in.

Before the four-day workweek movement, there were other programs that aimed to shift the focus from input to output. One was the results-only work environment, or ROWE, developed by Cali Ressler and Jody Thompson. Researchers Erin Kelly and her colleagues documented the implementation of a ROWE at the corporate headquarters of Best Buy.[30] The main goals of a ROWE are to refocus employees and managers on desired results, instead of how the work is done. At Best Buy, the initiative was implemented at the team level, with training and orientation sessions lasting about six hours. Employees and managers were first asked to critically examine their current work culture, then went through role-play exercises to practice how to respond to comments such as "Leaving early today, eh?" The trainers helped them identify phrases that do not reinforce the previous norms, such as "Is there something you need?" Finally, employees worked to identify specific practices they could change to support ROWE, such as ensuring coverage on projects to allow employees to take time off and implementing asynchronous forms of communication that allow for project flow even when employees aren't together.

Qualitative data from the initial training sessions revealed a strong ideal worker norm at Best Buy. You'll recognize many of these signals. There was widespread endorsement of the belief that long hours equaled dedication and productivity, which was evident in the reward system. Visible busyness was an indicator of status. Triple-booking yourself for meetings was seen as a sign that you were important. There was a focus on quick responsiveness.

Thus, it was not surprising skepticism quickly emerged about whether ROWE would work in the organization. Two departments that, not coincidentally, had the two loudest critics of the initiative, ultimately pulled out of ROWE during the research study.

But the data from departments that stuck with it clearly showed promise: decreased levels of work-family conflict, improvements in some health behaviors, such as sleep, and decreases in turnover.[31] The bad news: Best Buy pulled the plug on ROWE a few years later.[32] Ressler and Thompson went on to write about their experiences in *Why Work Sucks and How to Fix It* and later created CultureRx, a company that helps other companies implement ROWE.[33]

In addition to rewarding output instead of input, there are other traps that can be avoided. A classic management article highlights another trap: how our reward systems can actually motivate employees to do the opposite of what you want. Steve Kerr's classic article "The Folly of Rewarding A While Hoping for B" provides countless examples.[34] We hope for long-term growth, which may require short-term expenditures to build a proper foundation, but we reward quarterly earnings; we hope for teamwork, but reward individual effort. We hope for quality, but reward quantity.

Here's an example applicable to workaholism: your company touts its unlimited PTO to its new recruits and organizational stakeholders—but the people who move up in the organization are the ones who never take time off.

Break the Cycle of Responsiveness

In her book *Sleeping with Your Smartphone*, Leslie Perlow describes what she calls the cycle of responsiveness (see figure 5-1).[35] I will argue that this cycle is at the heart of any workaholic organization.

To illustrate the cycle, picture yourself starting a new job at an organization. As you go through your onboarding process, it becomes clear that you are expected to do whatever it takes to

FIGURE 5-1

Cycle of responsiveness: How genuine pressure to be *on* gets amplified through our own actions

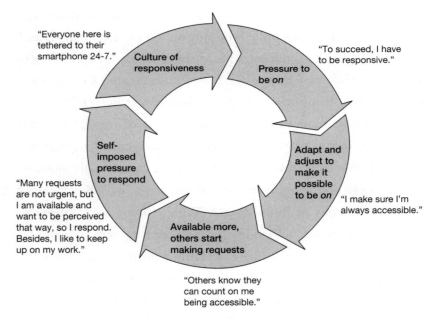

Source: Leslie A. Perlow, *Sleeping with Your Smartphone: How to Break the 24/7 Habit and Change the Way You Work* (Boston: Harvard Business Review Press, 2012).

meet a company goal—even if it means canceling personal plans or jumping on a flight at the last minute to take care of a problem. Also, your biggest client is in a different time zone, which means you need to adjust your normal hours to arrive at work early. You do not think much of this, as you are excited about your new job. And how bad can it really be?

As you settle into your new role, you realize that it's pretty common for your new boss to stroll into your office or send you an email around 4 p.m. with a request for something that he had promised your client they would get by tomorrow (the same client that's six hours ahead of you, so you are already behind before you start). You begin to anticipate this kind of request and start leaving the office later than you previously did so you aren't scrambling too much in the mornings. This means you have to skip your after-work workout, but . . . oh, well. You also work weekends to prepare for your Monday-morning team meetings. Once coworkers realize you're working anyway, they start sending weekend emails and texts, and you do the same with the people on your team. Before long, you start to become frustrated when you are *not* getting a response from one of your coworkers during those weekend work sessions, since it would be much easier if you could just wrap up the loose ends while everyone else was working on it: really, they are just making everyone else's jobs harder by not being available! You vow to not be that person, so you make sure to set up your phone so that emails come to you immediately. It helps you to stay on top of things, and it also makes you a good team player, you tell yourself.

Fast-forward one year, and you are now in charge of a small team that has just hired three new employees. You onboard them, and they notice right away, just as you did when you started, that they're expected to be available in your typical work patterns, including on the weekends. And thus, the cycle of responsiveness returns to the starting point again. In a year, they'll do the same.

Notice, too, that this workaholic trap emerged not from malfeasance or some deliberate scheme. People were trying to be helpful to each other and (they thought) to themselves in the context of a work devotion schema. Only all these small choices added up to workaholic behavior over time and then reinforcement of that behavior in others.

The cycle of responsiveness is detrimental to employee health and well-being and a strong reinforcer of a workaholic culture. A group of researchers conducted several studies examining the effects of organizational expectations for email monitoring on employees and their spouses.[36] They found that people who worked at organizations with high organizational expectations for connectivity experienced more frequent anxiety when they thought about their office contacting them after hours, and they showed overall poorer health. Additionally, their spouses experienced more anxiety because of it.

When I was working on this chapter, I happened to see a LinkedIn post from Emily, one of my former students, now an industrial-organizational practitioner in the talent management space. Emily started her post with the message, "Where you work matters!" That day was her first day back to work after taking a week and a half off for her wedding and honeymoon. She mentioned that she'd also been given a grace period to catch up on emails that she missed during her time off. Her team members stepped up to help with her responsibilities while she was away, and she received messages from coworkers asking how they could help her get back up to speed. "Not once was I worried about how much time off I was taking. Not once was I chastised for taking over a week off at one time. And not once did work blow up my phone!"

This is a great example of a company that is respecting time-off boundaries. But more than that, key members of the organization—her boss, her teammates—stepped up to take on additional responsibilities that would allow Emily to disconnect and enjoy this special moment in her life. What are some things your organization can do to make this happen? Will this involve cross-training employees? Integration of a shared mailbox so multiple employees can respond to an urgent customer request? Researchers Leslie Perlow and Jessica Porter call this process *teaming*—where individuals increase their shared responsibility for work to improve the ease with which they can cover for each other when needed.[37]

Another way to break the cycle of responsiveness is to change up how and when your team communicates with each other. Industrial-organizational psychologist Larissa Barber suggests three key strategies that can help combat this cycle of responsiveness:[38]

- Actively signal consideration of diverse work schedules and aim to reduce response urgency. Use "scheduled send" so emails do not arrive after hours or on weekends. Minimize the use of automatic notifications that send instant pings upon document sharing or uploading or message sending. Use shared documents or asynchronous platforms (e.g., Basecamp) for nonurgent tasks as opposed to email threads or chat-based communication platforms that will immediately "ping" the team.

- Coordinate activities for efficient interactions. Plan ahead and allow sufficient lead time for projects to avoid last-minute requests or impossible deadlines that require a mad scramble to meet a deadline. Send out key info or questions to consider before a scheduled meeting so everyone comes prepared and ready to dive into the details.

- Clarify expectations and reinforce ideal channels. Be specific in requests (who, what, when) and avoid vague requests such as "soon" or "at your earliest convenience." Discuss what qualifies as urgent versus nonurgent interruptions and appropriate channels for conveying messages that would fall into these categories (shared document, email, text, phone call).

Add Speed Bumps

As he sat in his office in Brooking Hall at Washington University, Arthur Compton became increasingly frustrated with the recklessness of the cars passing by his building. Not only was their driving dangerous for other vehicles, but also for pedestrians. So Compton created an ingenious device to fix the problem—what we now call a speed bump (or, in some places, a speed table). With his physics knowledge, he designed it perfectly so that it would damage a car only if it was driving recklessly.[39] Drivers learned quickly that slowing down beat the alternative.

Speed bumps are a great way for organizations to slow down workaholics. We already employ many. Engineer Fredrick Taylor, known as the founder of the principles of scientific management, implemented mandatory work breaks in his experiments with manual labor workers in a steel pig iron company.[40]

Research from industrial-organizational psychology shows that taking work breaks *before* you feel like you need them can be better for performance.[41] But there are other ideas, too. I spoke with Lauren Kuykendall, a professor of industrial-organizational psychology, about nudges, the behavioral science concept of subtly shaping behavior through environmental cues while still preserving people's freedom of choice.[42] On Chicago's Lake Shore Drive, drivers wind through a series of S curves. They offered great views, but were dangerous, and drivers often did not heed the warnings to reduce their speeds when taking these curves. To combat the high accident rate, the city painted a series of white stripes on the road that started off evenly spaced, but as drivers approached the most dangerous portion of the curve, the stripes were painted closer together. This optical illusion made it appear to drivers that their speed was increasing, which nudged them to brake as they approached the curve.

Nudges can be used to facilitate organizational interventions aiming to change patterns surrounding overwork, Kuykendall emphasized. One example is an automatic prompt if an employee attempts to send an email after work hours that asks, "It's after work hours. Are you sure you wish to send this?" Or, even better, maybe something like, "I noticed you are attempting to send this email after hours. Would you like to schedule this email to be sent at 8 a.m. tomorrow?" Another example is a message that pops up when employees are using their electronic devices during non-work time, gently reminding them they are not "on the clock." Or, to facilitate workplace breaks, the organization could paint footprints on the floor that lead outside to a walking path. We know nudges are effective. For example, in a randomized controlled trial involving thirty worksite cafeterias, nudges such as offering healthy products at the beginning of the route and offering a higher proportion of healthy options compared with less healthy options helped employees improve healthy eating behaviors.[43] We can learn from these studies to nudge employees to engage in healthier work patterns.

Lead by Example

A key way to ensure success of a workaholism-fighting change initiative is to focus on increasing supervisor support for recovery from high job demands and stress. Leaders must be clear with their messaging, but they also need to consistently demonstrate that they mean what they say through their own actions.

I again turn to my conversation with Lauren Kuykendall, an expert in recovery, and have used her work and my conversations with her to outline some of the lead-by-example practices that you can employ.

Supervisors should model non-workaholic behavior. It matters much less what you *say* as a leader of others, and much more what you *do*.

There are two levels to this. First is the lower level of everyday activities that reinforce a workaholic culture, often unintentionally. Remember that a well-intentioned message at the bottom of an email, indicating something like, "I may have different work hours than you, but feel free to respond during your regular work hours" still may be problematic. This is because leaders often suffer from what Kuykendall calls *status blindness*—a phenomenon where people in higher-level positions assume those with less power have the same amount of agency as they do. Drawing from the literature on power and social distance, Kuykendall and her colleagues argue that powerful people tend to enact their preferences, and lower-status people tend to conform to what's modeled by higher-status people.[44] In other words, just because a leader might be able to choose whether or not to respond to an urgent email or to stay at work to finish a project, this doesn't necessarily mean that individuals working underneath them will feel the same degree of power to make that decision. There might be too much pressure, due to company norms and expectations or due to the leader's influence over key rewards, that their subordinates don't feel they can wait to respond to that email, particularly if everyone else on the work team tends to respond immediately.

Supervisors can model rest and recovery during the workday (recall the research that shows work breaks are most effective *before* you are tired). Indeed, the research shows that when supervisors clearly indicate that these rest and recovery breaks are encouraged, employees are more likely to take them.[45]

Another classic example of modeling behavior comes around arrival and departure time. When there's no "work whistle" to signify the start and end of the day, people will conform to what the leaders do. They will also want to avoid being seen arriving later than others or leaving earlier.

At the second, higher level, are macro behaviors that must be well modeled. Do supervisors take all their vacation? Do they take parental leave? They may well have the financial means to overcome the need for extended leave by hiring professional in-home caretakers, for example. But by doing so, they are again implicitly pressuring people into overwork.

There are some classic examples of poor and positive modeling, even in an intensely workaholic industry like investment banking. On the one hand you have Byron Trott, a Goldman Sachs veteran and founder of his own firm, who puts in eighteen- to twenty-hour days.[46] Then again, you also have examples like Warren Buffett, who took his grandkids out for ice cream in the middle of a $5 billion investment negotiation.[47]

Beyond role-modeling with your own behaviors, it's also important to help your employees practice these behaviors when they fall back into the always-on trap. An example of this comes from my neighbor Jared, who works at a large light-fixture manufacturing company. Jared and his family had just returned from a seven-day vacation at the beach, and I was talking with him about how the trip was. The topic of workaholism came up. Although Jared doesn't identify as a workaholic, he admits that due to his role in the company as a project lead, sometimes he struggles with letting work go when he's doing other non-work things, such as his recent vacation. A few days into their trip, Jared decided to sit in on a work call with a supplier: "I feel like whenever I go on vacation, there's always something that comes up that demands my attention." Right now, it's a new product that Jared's team is bringing to market within the next month or two. "I decided to hop on the call because it was my kids' naptime, so I felt I wasn't missing out on much. And the call was pretty short. After the call, I emailed my boss to give him an update on how that meeting went. No response. After a couple of hours, I texted him. Twice. It's been days since that meeting, and I still haven't heard from him."

Reflecting on this, Jared fully knows what his boss will say when he returns to work on Monday—he shouldn't have been on that work call in the first place, because he was on vacation. Not responding to Jared's email and texts sends a clear message—when we say we want you to take a break from work, we mean it. Work should not be prioritized above that unless it's a dire emergency. "So, was it an emergency?" I asked Jared. "Not even close," he tells me. "I can just update him on Monday. Thinking about it more, I should have known better, and I appreciate my boss for reminding me of that."

The key here is discipline and consistency. Modeling good behavior must be so consistent that it becomes a new norm, and you can't send mixed messages. Brigid Schulte highlighted some of these mixed messages in our conversation: "You give somebody a lunchtime with yoga, but then you send them emails at ten o'clock at night. That's what you've got to address. Because if you do those wellness programs and then [also reinforce a 24-7 work atmosphere], you can actually create more cynicism. Basically you're modeling a trade-off. Sure, do your yoga, but then work at home to make up for it. Those signals must be eliminated."

Leaders should not create an amount of work and a deadline to complete it that forces people to work in non-work time. This is really where the workaholic clock error needs to be scrutinized. Spend some time gathering data on how often this is happening in your organization and how this is affecting your employee work patterns. Test your assumptions about the time it takes to complete work, using the method outlined in chapter 3. Increase your team's communication about the process—talk through how the work is getting done and who is doing what, when. This can help identify potential bottlenecks or cross-training opportunities that can be leveraged to support employees who take time off. Survey the workers. Implement new processes to assess the time needed to do tasks.

Leaders should communicate new models of high performance. As Alex Soojung-Kim Pang, author of the books *Shorter* and *Rest*, described to me, there is still a pervasive narrative that the only way to succeed and move up in one's career is to work sixty, seventy, eighty hours per week, especially in the early years of a career. Pang says that both active and passive messages reinforce this, and the way to change is to literally change the narrative around what it takes to be successful in an organization. Supervisors can do this by publicly recognizing people and connecting that to how the organization didn't suffer as a result. A group leader can call out Taylor, as she has figured out how to maximize her efficiency. She was able to land ten new accounts this month while rocking her four-day schedule. "If one of your employees figures out how to do something in four days that takes others five or six, that shouldn't be interpreted as a sign that they are less dedicated. It should be touted as a sign that your employee understands their work better than most. This is the kind of alternative narrative that needs to be emphasized by organizational leadership," Pang tells me.

An even more aggressive way to change the culture is to develop rewards around behaviors that are anti-workaholic. When analytics revealed to Chris Lovato, Medtronic's human capital insights director, that not enough people were using their vacation time, the company implemented a program called "Take time and win time." For each day of PTO employees took, they earned a ticket for a raffle to win a vacation getaway. Similarly, some companies like BambooHR actually *pay* their employees to go on vacations.[48]

You might be tempted to go in full bore and offer unlimited personal time off, treating it like a magic bullet for a workaholic culture. That won't work *unless the culture encourages rest*, which most don't. Unlimited time off can backfire and reinforce an overwork culture since there's no structure to it. The ambiguity around how much I'm *supposed to take* makes people not take it in an overwork culture. This idea plays out in the data. According to a *Forbes* article, even though the average American takes seventeen PTO days a year, workers who have unlimited PTO take only ten. Moreover, forty-two percent with unlimited PTO report always working on vacation.[49] If employees do not seem to be taking their allotted PTO days, companies could consider shifting to a "use it or lose it" PTO policy. When PTO is allowed to accumulate, it's easy to defer use of vacation time and tell yourself you'll take it another time, though data shows people don't end up doing that. On the other hand, as humans, we hate to lose out on something that is owed to us. Thus, if we are faced with the prospect of losing the vacation days that are not spent, people will be more likely to use them. Note that the use-it-or-lose-it policy *must* be paired with an organizational culture that is supportive of rest.

Predictable time off is another form of forced rest that has really been shown to be successful in demanding industries such as consulting, where the work devotion schema is very strong. At Boston Consulting Group, which had a strong 24-7 always on culture, researchers Leslie Perlow and Jessica Porter realized that a more drastic approach such as a four-day week was not something the organization would go for. Instead, they tried a more palatable trial: one mandated night of rest with no communication or work after the workday ended.[50] That predictable, required time off made their teams of consultants more productive.

Four Organizational To-Dos to Combat Workaholism

At a high level, the perfect storm for a toxic overwork culture is work intensity with high demands, strong norms of 24-7 connectivity, and low supervisor support for recovery. From that point of view, these are four to-dos the organization must do to combat workaholism.[51]

- Lower demands: Decrease work intensity and reset expectations on timelines and deadlines.

- Lower connectivity: Change norms related to how much workers are expected to be connected, when they are, and how responsive they're expected to be.

- Increase control: Give employees the autonomy to decide key components of their job, such as when they will (and will not) work.

- Increase support: Get leaders and supervisors to condone and reward non-workaholic behavior, both formally and informally.

I've offered many starting points for implementing these changes above. And still, I know there will be resistance at the organizational level, as I laid out at the start of this chapter. Despite evidence to the contrary, some leaders and organizations will not be able to easily escape their work devotion schema to see how counterproductive it is to encourage workaholism. They won't be able to draw the connections between flagging performance and their focus on a 24-7 culture. They won't see how the effects of workaholism create turnover costs, health-care costs, and productivity costs.

Most of all they won't believe that they can get the same output—indeed, better output—from fewer hours and less connectivity. It's just not intuitive.

But it's true. The research is clear. Work cultures that enable overwork are suboptimal. The Covid-19 pandemic was a major development in our realization that the work devotion schema may need adjusting. The success of four-day workweek trials was another.

More and more organizations see the value of changing their workaholic culture. You can, too. No more excuses.

Key Takeaways

- To disassemble a culture of overwork:

  - Find out what areas of your organization are in need of change through a culture assessment.

  - Plan for change. Carve out your purpose, build trust, design your experiment, and communicate clearly.

  - Start small.

- To drive actionable change:

  - Reward output, not input.

  - Break the cycle of responsiveness.

  - Add speed bumps.

  - Lead by example.

- To combat workaholism:

  - Adjust the intensity and urgency with which your employees are expected to work.

  - Change connectivity and responsiveness norms and expectations.

  - Provide employees with increased autonomy to decide how, when, and where they will work.

  - Formally and informally reward and model non-workaholic behavior.

CONCLUSION

Let's Resculpt

By now you should have a pretty good understanding of what workaholism is, its prevalence, and the factors that reinforce it. Maybe you have discovered that you have some workaholic tendencies yourself, or that you work for a workaholic boss. Perhaps you now recognize that your organization is sending overwork signals that contradict its stated values. I've also covered some research-backed strategies for kicking your own workaholic habits, as well as addressing the ways in which your organization might foster and reinforce an overwork culture.

And still, the most important message to take away from all of this is that the research conclusively strikes down the myth that workaholism is a good thing—for individuals, for their families, and, in particular, for their organizations. Workaholics suffer at the hands of their excessive and compulsive work, and those around them suffer as well. Workaholics are not more productive workers. Devotion to work—with our time, with our emotional energy, as our identity—does not result in better work output. Let's stop equating busyness with status, commitment, and productivity.

We continue to perpetuate the myth that long hours and devotion to work are indicative of performance because of the ever-present overwork norms that shape the norms and expectations of what it means to be the ideal worker. One woman I interviewed described this dilemma perfectly when she said, "Our culture does not acknowledge workaholism as a problem because it's like water to a fish." However, ignoring the problem is just as problematic as it would be to pour toxic chemicals into the water that fish breathe. Eventually, the fish suffocates.

We see the dangers of overwork and workaholism all around us, and we can't just pass off the blame to the workers themselves. Organizations (and societies) need to recognize the role they play in the problem.

Hopefully, this book has inspired your organization to take some actionable steps in fostering a healthier workplace. Marnie Dobson, director of the Healthy Work Campaign, urges organizations to stop trying to teach the worker to cope with the environment, and instead to focus on how the environment surrounding that worker can be changed. It's the same story as we tell with burnout—stop trying to put a Band-Aid on the problem by teaching mindfulness and other coping skills. Instead, focus on the source of the problem—the organizational factors that are contributing to that burnout in the first place. Coping is not a strategy; it's triage. It's not enough to fix the problem, only put it off.

The culture of overwork seems like a particularly American problem, with some Asian countries such as Japan, China, and South Korea also fostering a workaholic culture. And yet the research findings that showed workaholics are more likely to suffer a cardiovascular event, increased blood pressure, sleep problems, and heightened inflammatory response were collected from workers in Italy, the Netherlands, and Spain—countries hardly known for having workaholic cultures.[1]

It may be daunting to try to tackle a problem that seems as massive and systemic as this. It will not be easy or quick. It's also not something individuals can themselves fix, although the role of individuals in the larger organizational system are critical. The challenge will be to convince a critical mass of individuals—in particular, the individuals who have the authority to implement some organization-wide solutions—to start to move the needle. And this is where you come in.

Unsure where to begin? You could look to examples from the four-day workweek trials, or Cali Ressler and Jody Thompson's results-only work environment. Look at initiatives such as the Healthy Work Campaign or the National Institute for Occupational Safety and Health's Total Worker Health initiative. Look to steps that some countries have taken; for example, in 2017, the French government implemented a "right to disconnect" law—a legal requirement for employers with more than fifty employees to set out hours when staff are forbidden from sending or answering emails.

When you think about implementing these changes in your organization, meet people where they are, but also push them to go further than they believed they could go. If the leadership team seems offended at the concept of the four-day workweek, consider starting with small changes, such as the predictable time-off experiment at Boston Consulting Group. At the same time, remember that change cannot happen if people don't step out of their comfort zone, so push for experiments that challenge the organization to adapt and change. Figure out what you can do to help your organization shift from "always on" to "optimally on."[2] Shifting an organizational culture is undoubtedly a huge change for many organizations, so resistance is not unexpected. Indeed, research indicates that ambivalence often encourages change by keeping the conversation going.[3]

The Covid-19 pandemic has exposed the fallacy of the ideal worker norm. At the height of the pandemic, when schools were virtual, parents who previously been able to hide their family responsibilities from their work had kids running around in the background of Zoom calls. For some, this was the first time their coworkers had seen their lives outside of the workplace. Many leaders were applauded for their candid statements about how they too struggled with some of the same issues. There are signs we are slowly shedding the old-fashioned ideas of what it means to be a good father. Before, being a good father equated to being the family provider. The more money he brought home, the better father he was. However, men today are more likely than ever to proudly engage in childrearing. As Joan Williams notes in her *Harvard Business Review* article, "If there was ever a time to put to rest the old-fashioned notion of the ideal worker, it's now. Postpandemic, let's resculpt workplace ideals so they reflect people's lives today—not half a century ago."[4] I couldn't agree more.

Let's start a conversation of what the new "ideal worker" should be. While we're on the topic, let's talk about what the "ideal workplace" should be as well. It is possible for organizations to be wildly successful when they value both productivity *and* the health and well-being of workers.

Writing this book has inspired me to make some changes in my own life, both for my own workaholic tendencies and also to help move the needle more broadly by practicing what I preach. I've told my research lab we'll be switching our lab communications from a synchronous communication platform (Slack) to an asynchronous one (Basecamp). I've also started to use the "schedule send" option in Microsoft Outlook more often, particularly when I'm communicating with my graduate students. Even with all this, I know I have a long way to go—I am still battling my workaholic tendencies to check my work email at all hours of the day, for example. Hopefully, over time, I will be able to work on that as well.

I urge you to do the same. Start to make change. Don't wait for others. You can do this. And if enough of you do, we'll chip away at the work devotion schema and begin to shape something different, a new normal. Find just one thing to address your own workaholic tendencies, or just one way you could reduce your organization's workaholic culture. Then find another. And another. Chip away at it. Imagine what kind of workplace you would want your children or future generations of workers to experience. Keep chipping away, and soon enough, you'll see that better future, the resculpted world of work, start to emerge.

Overwork Assessments

Multidimensional Workaholism Scale

The MWS captures the motivational, cognitive, emotional, and behavioral dimensions of workaholism. There are four items per dimension. Total scores can range from 16 to 80. A good rule of thumb is that if your total score is 60 or above, you could be considered a workaholic.

Instructions: Please indicate the degree to which each item describes you using the following scale:

---

1 = never true   2 = seldom true   3 = sometimes true
4 = often true   5 = always true

Dimension	Item	Your score
Motivational	I always have an inner pressure inside of me that drives me to work.	
	I work because there is a part inside of me that feels compelled to work.	
	I have a strong inner desire to work all of the time.	
	There is a pressure inside of me that drives me to work.	
Cognitive	I feel like I cannot stop myself from thinking about working.	
	In general, I spend my free time thinking about work.	
	At any given time, the majority of my thoughts are work-related.	
	It is difficult for me to stop thinking about work when I stop working.	
Emotional	I feel upset if I have to miss a day of work for any reason.	
	I am almost always frustrated when I am not able to work.	
	I feel upset if I cannot continue to work.	
	When something prevents me from working, I usually get agitated.	
Behavioral	When most of my coworkers will take breaks, I keep working.	
	I work more than what is expected of me.	
	I tend to work longer hours than most of my coworkers.	
	I tend to work beyond my job's requirements.	
	Total score:	

Source: Malissa A. Clark, Rachel Williamson Smith, and Nicholas J. Haynes, "The Multidimensional Workaholism Scale: Linking the Conceptualization and Measurement of Workaholism," *Journal of Applied Psychology* 105, no. 11 (2020): 1281–1307, https://doi.org/10.1037/apl0000484.

Workaholics Anonymous 20 Questions

According to Workaholics Anonymous, if you answer yes to three or more of the following questions, you may have a problem with workaholism.

1. Are you more drawn to your work or activity than close relationships, rest, etc.?

2. Are there times when you are motivated and push through tasks when you do not even want to and other times when you procrastinate and avoid them when you would prefer to get things done?

3. Do you take work with you to bed? On weekends? On vacation?

4. Are you more comfortable talking about your work than other topics?

5. Do you pull all-nighters?

6. Do you resent your work or people at your workplace for imposing so many pressures on you?

7. Do you avoid intimacy with others and/or yourself?

8. Do you resist rest when tired and use stimulants to stay awake longer?

9. Do you take on extra work or volunteer commitments because you are concerned that things will not otherwise get done?

10. Do you regularly underestimate how long something will take and then rush to complete it?

11. Do you immerse yourself in activities to change how you feel or avoid grief, anxiety, and shame?

12. Do you get impatient with people who have other priorities besides work?

13. Are you afraid that if you do not work hard all the time, you will lose your job or be a failure?

14. Do you fear success, failure, criticism, burnout, financial insecurity, or not having enough time?

15. Do you try to multitask to get more done?

16. Do you get irritated when people ask you to stop doing what you are doing in order to do something else?

17. Have your long hours caused injury to your health or relationships?

18. Do you think about work or other tasks while driving, conversing, falling asleep, or sleeping?

19. Do you feel agitated when you are idle and/or hopeless that you will ever find balance?

20. Do you feel like a slave to your email, texts, or other technology?

Source: Reprinted from *The Workaholics Anonymous Book of Recovery*, 2nd ed. (Menlo Park, CA: Workaholics Anonymous World Service Organization, 2015), 2–3, with the permission of Workaholics Anonymous World Services Organization. Copyrighted material may not be reproduced in any form without the written permission of the WAWSO.

NOTES

Introduction

1. Unless otherwise noted, quotations are from interviews and personal conversations conducted by the author between July 2021 and March 2023.

2. George Fink, "Stress: Concepts, Definition and History," in *Reference Module in Neuroscience and Biobehavioral Psychology*, ed. John Stein (Amsterdam: Elsevier, 2017), 1–9.

3. "U.S. Employees Working More Hours during COVID-19 Pandemic," Business Facilities, March 23, 2020, https://businessfacilities.com/u-s-employees-working-more-hours-during-covid-19-pandemic.

4. Jared Spataro, "The Future of Work—The Good, the Challenging and the Unknown," *Microsoft 365* (blog), July 8, 2020, https://www.microsoft.com/en-us/microsoft-365/blog/2020/07/08/future-work-good-challenging-unknown/; "The Rise of the Triple Peak Day," *Microsoft 365* (blog), n.d., https://www.microsoft.com/en-us/worklab/triple-peak-day.

5. OECD Family Database, https://www.oecd.org/els/family/database.htm; several US states have a paid leave mandate at the *state* level, including California, New Jersey, New York, Rhode Island, Washington, and the District of Columbia. This statement is referring to legislation at the national level.

6. Niha Masih, "Tired of After-Work Emails and Calls? In These Countries, They're Outlawed," *Washington Post*, February 1, 2023, https://www.washingtonpost.com/business/2023/02/01/right-to-disconnect-laws/.

7. Andrea Hsu, "Iceland Cut Its Work Week and Found Greater Happiness and No Loss in Productivity," NPR, July 6, 2021, https://www.npr.org/2021/07/06/1013348626/iceland-finds-major-success-moving-to-shorter-work-week.

8. See, for example, the four-day week movement. Andrew Barnes, *The 4 Day Week: How the Flexible Work Revolution Can Increase Productivity, Profitability and Well-Being, and Create a Sustainable Future* (London: Piatkus, 2020); Alex Soojung-Kim Pang, *Shorter: Work Better, Smarter, and Less—Here's How* (New York: PublicAffairs, 2020).

9. Charlotte Huff, "Employers Are Increasing Support for Mental Health," *Monitor on Psychology* 52, no. 1 (January 1, 2021), https://www.apa.org/monitor /2021/01/trends-employers-support.

10. See, for example, the *National Institute for Occupational Safety and Health's Worker Well-Being Questionnaire* (NIOSH WellBQ), Centers for Disease Control and Prevention, revised August 4, 2021, https://www.cdc.gov/niosh/twh/wellbq /default.html.

Chapter 1

1. Charlie Giattino, Esteban Ortiz-Ospina, and Max Roser, "Are We Working More Than Ever?" Working Hours, Our World in Data, 2013, rev. December 2020, https://ourworldindata.org/working-hours#are-we-working -more-than-ever. It should be noted that depending on how you analyze hours worked, you may hear different conclusions being drawn about whether hours worked have increased or decreased. For example, if you compare annual hours worked in the 2010s to the 1970s, you will find an increase of over 180 hours. However, much of that increase reflects a shift in worker demographics as opposed to increases in work hours, per se. In other words, the increase in hours noted between those two time periods seems to be reflective of women increasing their participation in the paid labor force. For a discussion of these analyses, see Lawrence Mishel, *Vast Majority of Wage Earners Are Working Harder, and for Not Much More* (Washington, DC: Economic Policy Institute, 2013).

2. Giattino, Ortiz-Ospina, and Roser, "Are We Working More Than Ever?"

3. Vivian Giang, "How Everything We Tell Ourselves About How Busy We Are Is a Lie," *Fast Company*, September 15, 2014, https://www.fastcompany .com/3035253/how-everything-we-tell-ourselves-about-how-busy-we-are-is -a-lie.

4. Juliet B. Schor et al., *The Four Day Week: Assessing Global Trials of Reduced Work Time with No Reduction in Pay* (Auckland, NZ: 4 Day Week Global, 2022).

5. Tyler Schmidt, "Almost Half of Americans Consider Themselves Workaholics," *New York Post*, February 1, 2019, https://nypost.com/2019/02/01 /almost-half-of-americans-consider-themselves-workaholics/.

6. "The Workaholism Issue: Millennials Work Too Much," *Morning Future* (blog), Adecco Group, July 24, 2019, https://www.morningfuture.com/en/2019 /07/24/workaholism-millennials-work/.

7. "Paid Time Off Trends in the U.S.," U.S. Travel Association, n.d., https:// www.ustravel.org/sites/default/files/media_root/document/Paid%20Time%20 Off%20Trends%20Fact%20Sheet.pdf.

8. Malissa A. Clark et al., "All Work and No Play? A Meta-Analytic Examination of the Correlates and Outcomes of Workaholism," *Journal of Management* 42, no. 7 (2016): 1836–1873, https://doi.org/10.1177 /0149206314522301; Marisa Salanova et al., "Your Work May Be Killing You! Workaholism, Sleep Problems and Cardiovascular Risk," *Work and Stress* 30,

no. 3 (2016): 228–242, https://doi.org/10.1080/02678373.2016.1203373; Damiano Girardi et al., "Is Workaholism Associated with Inflammatory Response? The Moderating Role of Work Engagement," *TPM-Testing, Psychometrics, Methodology in Applied Psychology* 26, no. 2 (2019): 305–322, https://doi.org/10.4473 /TPM26.2.9.

9. Alessandra Falco et al., "The Mediating Role of Psychophysics Strain in the Relationship between Workaholism, Job Performance, and Sickness Absence: A Longitudinal Study," *Journal of Occupational and Environmental Medicine* 55, no. 11 (2013): 1255–1261, https://doi.org/10.1097/JOM.0000000000000007; Narhee Kim et al., "The Crossover Effects of Supervisors' Workaholism on Subordinates' Turnover Intention: The Mediating Role of Two Types of Job Demands and Emotional Exhaustion," *International Journal of Environmental Research and Public Health* 17, no. 21 (2020): 7742, https://doi.org/10.3390/ijerph17217742; Marjan Gorgievski, Juan A. Moriano, and Arnold B. Bakker, "Relating Work Engagement and Workaholism to Entrepreneurial Performance," *Journal of Managerial Psychology* 29, no. 2 (2014): 106–121, http://dx.doi.org/10.1108/JMP-06 -2012-0169; Diana Wilkie, "Workaholics: Job 'Addicts' Can Hurt Selves, Morale, Company," *The SHRM Blog*, July 17, 2014, https://blog.shrm.org/workplace /workaholics-job-addicts-can-hurt-selves-morale-company.

10. In a 2016 meta-analysis, my colleagues and I found that workaholism and work hours were only moderately correlated (r = .30); Clark et al., "All Work and No Play?"

11. "Death from Overwork in China," *China Labour Bulletin*, August 11, 2006, https://clb.org.hk/content/death-overwork-china.

12. Cristian Balducci, Lorenzo Avanzi, and Franco Fraccaroli, "The Individual 'Costs' of Workaholism: An Analysis Based on Multisource and Prospective Data," *Journal of Management* 44, no. 7 (2018): 2961–2986, https://doi .org/10.1177/0149206316658348; Lieke L. ten Brummelhuis, Nancy P. Rothbard, and Benjamin Uhrich, "Beyond Nine to Five: Is Working to Excess Bad for Health?" *Academy of Management Discoveries* 3, no. 3 (2017): 262–283, https://doi .org/10.5465/amd.2015.0115; Salanova et al., "Your Work May Be Killing You!"

13. Christina Maslach, "Job Burnout: New Directions in Research and Intervention," *Current Directions in Psychological Science* 12, no. 5 (2003): 189–192, https://doi.org/10.1111/1467-8721.01258.

14. Clark et al., "All Work and No Play?"

15. Clark et al., "All Work and No Play?"; ten Brummelhuis, Rothbard, and Uhrich, "Beyond Nine to Five."

16. Jessica Stillman, "Why You Shouldn't Be Proud to Be a Workaholic," *Inc.*, November 11, 2014, https://www.inc.com/jessica-stillman/why-you-shouldn-t-be -proud-to-be-a-workaholic.html.

17. Richard M. Ryan and Edward L. Deci, "Self-Determination Theory and the Facilitation of Intrinsic Motivation, Social Development, and Well-Being," *American Psychologist* 55, no. 1 (2000): 68–78, https://doi.org/10.1037//0003 -066x.55.1.68.

18. Maryléne Gagné and Edward L. Deci, "Self-Determination Theory and Work Motivation," *Journal of Organizational Behavior* 26, no. 4 (2005): 331–362, https://doi.org/10.1002/job.322.

19. Toon W. Taris, Wilmar B. Scheufeli, and Akhito Shimazu, "The Push and Pull of Work: The Differences between Workaholism and Work Engagement," in *Work Engagement: A Handbook of Essential Theory and Research*, eds. Arnold B. Bakker and Michael P. Leiter (Washington, DC: Psychology Press. 2010), 39–53.

20. Paul Hemp, "Presenteeism: At Work—but Out of It," *Harvard Business Review*, October 2004.

21. Kristina A. Bourne and Pamela J. Forman, "Living in a Culture of Overwork: An Ethnographic Study of Flexibility," *Journal of Management Inquiry* 23, no. 1 (March 2013): 68–79, https://doi.org/10.1177/1056492613481245.

Chapter 2

1. Joel Goh, Jeffrey Pfeffer, and Stefanos A. Zenios, "Workplace Stressors and Health Outcomes: Health Policy for the Workplace," *Behavioral Science and Policy Association*, February 15, 2017, 43–52, https://behavioralpolicy.org/articles/workplace-stressors-health-outcomes-health-policy-for-the-workplace/.

2. Slate, "American Karoshi—The Problem with Work Stress," *Better Life Lab*, podcast, March 29, 2022, https://slate.com/podcasts/better-life-lab/2022/03/work-stress-karoshi.

3. Jack Austen Hassell, *Workaholic Stories: A Qualitative Exploration of the Lived Experience of Workaholism* (PhD diss., University of Canterbury, 2023), https://ir.canterbury.ac.nz/server/api/core/bitstreams/a64c8253-7843-4fc4-afbf-e0684f70ac20/content.

4. Malissa A. Clark, Rachel Williamson Smith, and Nicholas J. Haynes, "The Multidimensional Workaholism Scale: Linking the Conceptualization and Measurement of Workaholism," *Journal of Applied Psychology* 105, no. 11 (2020): 1281–1307, https://doi.org/10.1037/apl0000484.

5. Malissa A. Clark, Jesse S. Michel, and Boris B. Baltes, "All Work and No Play? A Meta-Analytic Examination of the Correlates and Outcomes of Workaholism," *Journal of Management* 42, no. 7 (2016): 1836–1873, https://doi.org/10.1177/0149206314522301.

6. Hans Selye, "Stress and Disease," *Science* 122 (1955): 625–631, https://doi.org/10.1126/science.122.3171.625.

7. Jeff Wise, "When Fear Makes Us Superhuman," *Scientific American*, December 28, 2009, https://www.scientificamerican.com/article/extreme-fear-superhuman/.

8. Daniel C. Ganster, "Work Stress and Employee Health: A Multidisciplinary Review," *Journal of Management* 39, no. 5, https://doi.org/10.1177/0149206313475815.

9. Robert-Paul Juster, Bruce S. McEwen, and Sonia J. Lupien, "Allostatic Load Biomarkers of Chronic Stress and Impact on Health and Cognition,"

Neuroscience Biobehavioral Review 35, no. 1 (2010): 2–16, https://doi.org/10.1016/j
.neubiorev.2009.10.002.

10. John H. Pencavel, *Diminishing Returns at Work: The Consequences of Long
Working Hours* (New York: Oxford University Press, 2018).

11. Akizumi Tsutsumi, "Prevention and Management of Work-Related
Cardiovascular Disorders," *International Journal of Occupational Medicine and
Environmental Health* 28, no. 1 (2015): 4–7, http://ijomeh.eu/Prevention-and
-management-of-work-related-cardiovascular-disorders,1940,0,2.html.

12. Marianna Virtanen et al., "Overtime Work and Incident Coronary Heart
Disease: The Whitehall II Prospective Cohort Study," *European Heart Journal* 31,
no. 14 (July 2010): 1737–1744, https://academic.oup.com/eurheartj/article
/31/14/1737/436396.

13. Pencavel, *Diminishing Returns at Work*.

14. Haiou Yang et al., "Work Hours and Self-Reported Hypertension among
Working People in California," *Hypertension* 48, no. 4 (2006): 744–750, https://
doi.org/10.1161/01.HYP.0000238327.41911.52; Alexis Descatha et al., "The Effect
of Exposure to Long Working Hours on Stroke: A Systematic Review and Meta-
Analysis from the WHO/ILO Joint Estimates of the Work-Related Burden of
Disease and Injury," *Environment International* 142 (2020): 105746, https://doi
.org/10.1016/j.envint.2020.105746.

15. Lieke L. ten Brummelhuis, Nancy P. Rothbard, and Benjamin Uhrich,
"Beyond Nine to Five: Is Working to Excess Bad for Health?" *Academy of
Management Discoveries* 3, no. 3 (2017): 262–283, https://doi.org/10.5465/amd
.2015.0115.

16. Marisa Salanova et al., "Your Work May Be Killing You! Workaholism,
Sleep Problems and Cardiovascular Risk," *Work and Stress* 30, no. 3 (2016): 228–242,
https://doi.org/10.1080/02678373.2016.1203373.

17. Cristian Balducci et al., "A Within-Individual Investigation on the
Relationship between Day Level Workaholism and Systolic Blood Pressure,"
Work and Stress 36, no. 4 (2022): 337–354, https://doi.org/10.1080/02678373.2021
.1976883.

18. Camille Zenobia and George Hajishengallis, "Basic Biology and Role of
Interleukin-17 in Immunity and Inflammation," *Periodontology* 69, no. 1 (2015):
142–159, https://doi.org/10.1111/prd.12083.

19. Junjie Zhao, "The Role of Interleukin-17 in Tumor Development and
Progression," special collection, *Journal of Experimental Medicine, JEM 2020
Update on Cancer Immunology and Immunotherapy* 217, no. 1 (2020):
e20190297, https://doi.org/10.1084/jem.20190297.

20. Damiano Girardi et al., "Is Workaholism Associated with Inflammatory
Response? The Moderating Role of Work Engagement," *TPM-Testing, Psychometrics,
Methodology in Applied Psychology* 26, no. 2 (2019): 305–322, https://doi.org/10.4473
/TPM26.2.9.

21. Salanova et al., "Your Work May Be Killing You!"

22. Salanova et al., "Your Work May Be Killing You!"

23. Clark, Smith, and Hayes, "The Multidimensional Workaholism Scale"; Marianna Virtanen et al., "Overtime Work as a Predictor of Major Depressive Episode: A 5-Year Follow-Up of the Whitehall II Study," *PLOS ONE* 7, no. 1 (2012), e30719.

24. Danielle De La Mare, "Addiction, Academic Women, [and Choosing Wellness] with Dr. Lauren Broyles," *Self-Compassionate Professor*, podcast, episode 129, August 17, 2022, https://podcasters.spotify.com/pod/show/danielle-de-la -mare/episodes/129--Addiction--academic-women--and-choosing-wellness -with-Dr--Lauren-Broyles-e1mjra7; Mandy Saligari, "Feelings: Handle Them Before They Handle You," TEDxGuildford, May 2017, https://www.youtube .com/watch?v=JD4O7ama3o8.

25. Bryan E. Robinson, *Chained to the Desk: A Guidebook for Workaholics, Their Partners and Children, and the Clinicians Who Treat Them* (New York: NYU Press, 2014).

Chapter 3

1. Paul Raeburn, "Arianna Huffington: Collapse from Exhaustion Was 'Wake-Up Call,'" *Today*, May 9, 2014, https://www.today.com/health /arianna-huffington-collapse-exhaustion-was-wake-call-2d79644042.

2. Bronnie Ware, *The Top Five Regrets of the Dying* (Carlsbad, CA: Hay House, 2019).

3. Shane Frederick, George Loewenstein, and Ted Donoghue, "Time Discounting and Time Preference: A Critical Review," *Journal of Economic Literature* 40, no. 2 (2002): 351–401, https://doi.org/10.1257/002205102320161311.

4. Ashley Whillans, *Time Smart: How to Reclaim Your Time and Live a Happier Life* (Boston: Harvard Business Review Press, 2020).

5. Dan Siegel, "Name It to Tame It," YouTube video, December 8, 2014, https://www.youtube.com/watch?v=ZcDLzppD4Jc.

6. *Workaholics Anonymous Book of Discovery* (Menlo Park, CA: Workaholics Anonymous World Services Organization, 2010).

7. Darria Long, "An ER Doctor on Triaging Your 'Crazy Busy' Life," TEDxNaperville, November 2019, https://www.ted.com/talks/darria_long_an_er _doctor_on_triaging_your_crazy_busy_life.

8. Robert G. Lord et al., "Self-Regulation at Work," *Annual Review of Psychology* 61 (2010): 543–568, https://doi.org/10.1146/annurev.psych.093008 .100314.

9. Vincent Phan and James W. Beck, "Why Do People (Not) Take Breaks? An Investigation of Individuals' Reasons for Taking and for Not Taking Breaks at Work," *Journal of Business and Psychology* 38 (2023): 259–282, https://doi.org /10.1007/s10869-022-09866-4.

10. "The Eisenhower Matrix," Todoist app, https://todoist.com/productivity -methods/eisenhower-matrix.

11. Long, "An ER Doctor on Triaging Your 'Crazy Busy' Life."

12. I had the pleasure of interviewing Adam Grant when I was the Division 14 Program Chair for a keynote titled "Fireside Chat with Adam Grant," at the

American Psychological Association Convention, August 2021. Many of the quotations used in this chapter come from that conversation.

13. Adam Grant, When Work Takes Over Your Life," TED, April 2018, https://www.ted.com/talks/worklife_with_adam_grant_when_work_takes _over_your_life.

14. Roger Buehler, Dale Griffin, and Michael Ross, "Exploring the 'Planning Fallacy': Why People Underestimate Their Task Completion Times," *Journal of Personality and Social Psychology* 67, no. 3 (1994): 366–381, https://doi.org/10.1037 /0022-3514.67.3.366.

15. E. J. Masicampo and Roy F. Baumeister, "Consider It Done! Plan Making Can Eliminate the Cognitive Effects of Unfulfilled Goals," *Journal of Personality and Social Psychology* 101, no. 4 (2011): 667–683, https://doi.org/10.1037/a0024192.

16. Brandon W. Smit and Larissa K. Barber, "Psychologically Detaching Despite High Workloads: The Role of Attentional Processes," *Journal of Occupational Health Psychology* 21, no. 4 (2016): 432–442, https://doi.org/10.1037 /ocp0000019.

17. Sabine Sonnentag, Laura Venz, and Anne Casper, "Advances in Recovery Research: What Have We Learned? What Should Be Done Next?" *Journal of Occupational Health Psychology* 22, no. 3 (2017): 365–380, http://dx.doi.org /10.1037/ocp0000079.

18. Emily M. Hunter and Cindy Wu, "Give Me a Better Break: Choosing Workday Break Activities to Maximize Resource Recovery," *Journal of Applied Psychology* 101, no. 2 (2016): 302–311, http://dx.doi.org/10.1037/apl0000045.

19. Sonnentag, Venz, and Casper, "Advances in Recovery Research."

20. Arnold B. Bakker et al., "Workaholism and Daily Recovery: A Day Reconstruction Study of Leisure Activities," *Journal of Organizational Behavior* 34, no. 4 (2013): 87–107, https://doi.org/10.1002/job.1796.

21. Andrew A. Bennett, "Better Together? Examining Profiles of Employee Recovery Experiences," *Journal of Applied Psychology* 101, no. 12 (2016): 1635–1654, https://doi.org/10.1037/apl0000157.

22. Sabine Sonnentag and Charlotte Fritz, "The Recovery Experience Questionnaire: Development and Validation of a Measure for Assessing Recuperation and Unwinding from Work," *Journal of Occupational Health Psychology* 12, no. 3 (July 2007): 204–221, https://doi.org/10.1037/1076-8998.12.3.204.

23. Charles Calderwood et al., "Understanding the Relationship between Prior to End-of-Workday Physical Activity and Work–Life Balance: A Within-Person Approach," *Journal of Applied Psychology* 106, no. 8 (2021): 1239–1249, http://dx.doi.org/10.1037/apl0000829.

Chapter 4

1. For this historical account, I relied heavily on a couple of fantastic sources: Celeste Headlee, *Do Nothing: How to Break Away from Overworking, Overdoing, and Underliving* (New York: Harmony Books, 2020); and Juliet Schor, *The Overworked American: The Unexpected Decline of Leisure* (New York: Basic Books, 1991).

2. Headlee, *Do Nothing*, 25

3. Frederick Douglass, "Self-Made Men" (lecture, 1872, first delivered 1859), https://monadnock.net/douglass/self-made-men.html.

4. Headlee, *Do Nothing*, 40.

5. Schor, *The Overworked American*.

6. OECD Family Database, "PF2.3: Additional Leave Entitlements for Working Parents," OECD, January 2020, https://www.oecd.org/els/soc /PF2_3_Additional_leave_entitlements_of_working_parents.pdf.

7. Kushboo Seth, "Countries with the Most Public Holidays," World Atlas, October 1, 2018, https://www.worldatlas.com/articles/countries-with-the-most -public-holidays.html.

8. Schor, *The Overworked American*.

9. "Because Americans Still Need to Take All Their Time Off," US Travel Association, https://www.ustravel.org/sites/default/files/media_root/document /NPVD19_FactSheet.pdf.

10. Gary S. Becker, "A Theory of the Allocation of Time," *Economic Journal* 75, no. 299 (1965): 493–517, https://doi.org/10.2307/2228949.

11. Mary Blair-Loy, *Competing Devotions: Career and Family among Women Executives* (Cambridge, MA: Harvard University Press, 2003).

12. Erin A. Cech, *The Trouble with Passion: How Searching for Fulfillment at Work Fosters Inequality* (Oakland, CA: University of California Press, 2021); Christine M. Beckman and Melissa Mazmanian, *Dreams of the Overworked: Living, Working, and Parenting in the Digital Age* (Stanford, CA: Stanford University Press, 2020); Blair-Loy, *Competing Devotions*.

13. Marcum LLP advertisement, YouTube video, May 18, 2022, https://www .youtube.com/watch?v=YzPI9e-fKKM.

14. Erin L. Kelly et al., "Gendered Challenge, Gendered Response: Confronting the Ideal Worker Norm in a White-Collar Organization," *Gender and Society* 24, no. 3 (2010): 281–303, https://doi.org/10.1177/0891243210372.

15. Benjamin Schneider et al., "Organizational Climate and Culture: Reflections on the History of the Constructs in the *Journal of Applied Psychology*," *Journal of Applied Psychology* 102, no. 3 (March 2017): 468–482, https://doi.org /10.1037/apl0000090.

16. Benjamin Schneider, "The People Make the Place," *Personnel Psychology* 40, no. 3 (September 1987): 437–453, https://doi.org/10.1111/j.1744-6570.1987 .tb00609.x.

17. Edgar A. Schein, with Peter A. Schein, *Organizational Culture and Leadership*, 5th ed. (Hoboken, NJ: John Wiley & Sons, 2016).

18. Menlo Innovations, "Who We Are," https://menloinnovations.com /our-way/our-people.

19. Andy Hertzfeld, "90 Hours a Week and Loving It!" *Folklore* (Apple blog), October 1983, https://www.folklore.org/StoryView.py?story=90_Hours_A_Week _And_Loving_It.txt.

20. Research Live, "What's the Mandarin for 'Work/Life Balance'?" October 20, 2011, https://www.research-live.com/article/opinion/whats-the-mandarin-for-worklife-balance/id/4006242.

21. Associated Press, "Coughlin: 'Meetings Start Five Minutes Early,'" September 13, 2004, https://www.espn.com/nfl/news/story?id=1881006.

22. Kate Aronoff, "Thank God It's Monday," *Dissent*, Winter 2017, https://www.dissentmagazine.org/article/wework-sharing-economy-labor-company-town.

23. Eliot Brown and Maureen Farrell, *The Cult of We: WeWork, Adam Neumann, and the Great Startup Delusion* (New York: Crown, 2021).

24. Manisha Thakor, *MoneyZen: The Secret to Finding Your "Enough"* (New York: Harper Business, 2023).

25. Adam Grant, "The 4 Deadly Sins of Work Culture," in *WorkLife with Adam Grant*, podcast, June 21, 2022, https://podcasts.apple.com/us/podcast/the-4-deadly-sins-of-work-culture/id1346314086?i=1000567259056.

26. Sara Ashley O'Brien, "Marissa Mayer on Maternity Leave: 'I Understand I'm the Exception,'" CNN Money, May 6, 2016, https://money.cnn.com/2016/05/06/technology/yahoo-marissa-mayer-maternity-leave/index.html.

27. Sophie Kleeman, "Marissa Mayer: You, Too, Can Work 130 Hours a Week If You Plan When to Take a Shit," Gizmodo, August 4, 2016, https://gizmodo.com/marissa-mayer-you-too-can-work-130-hours-a-week-if-y-1784822446.

28. Simone Arbour et al., "Person-Organization Fit: Using Normative Behaviors to Predict Workplace Satisfaction, Stress and Intentions to Stay," *Journal of Organizational Culture, Communications and Conflict* 18, no. 1 (2014): 41–64; Larissa K. Barber and Alecia M. Santuzzi, "Please Respond ASAP: Workplace Telepressure and Employee Recovery," *Journal of Occupational Health Psychology* 20, no. 2 (2015): 172–189, https://doi.org/10.1037/a0038278.

29. "Hawthorne Effect," http://www.analytictech.com/mb021/handouts/bank_wiring.htm; "Hawthorne Experiments," *Encyclopedia of Business*, 2nd ed., https://www.referenceforbusiness.com/encyclopedia/Gov-Inc/Hawthorne-Experiments.html.

30. Thanks to professor Marcus Dickson, who told us this story in 2005 in our graduate research methods class.

31. Cali Ressler and Jody Thompson, *Why Work Sucks and How to Fix It: No Schedules, No Meetings, No Joke—the Simple Change That Can Make Your Job Terrific* (New York: Portfolio, 2008), 47.

32. Wondery, "Thank God It's Monday," in *WeCrashed*, podcast, March 14, 2022, https://wondery.com/shows/we-crashed/season/1/.

33. Benjamin Schneider et al., "Organizational Climate and Culture: Reflections on the History of the Constructs," *Journal of Applied Psychology* 102, no. 3 (2017): 468–482, https://doi.org/10.1037/apl0000090; Schein and Schein, *Organizational Culture and Leadership*.

34. Adam Grant, LinkedIn.com, 2021, https://www.linkedin.com /posts/adammgrant_the-most-direct-way-to-figure-out-whats-activity -6796413238000054273-zIPB?utm_source=linkedin_share&utm_medium =member_desktop_web.

35. Erin Griffith, "Why Are Young People Pretending to Love Work?" *New York Times*, January 26, 2019, https://www.nytimes.com/2019/01/26/business /against-hustle-culture-rise-and-grind-tgim.html.

36. Steve Gruenert and Todd Whitaker, *School Culture Rewired: How to Define, Assess, and Transform It* (Alexandria, VA: ASCD, 2015).

37. Albert Bandura, Dorothea Ross, and Sheila A. Ross, "Transmission of Aggression through Imitation of Aggressive Models," *Journal of Abnormal and Social Psychology* 63, no. 3 (1961): 575–582, https://doi.org/10.1037/h0045925.

38. Melissa Mazmanian, Joanne Yates, and Wanda Orlikowski, "Ubiquitous Email: Individual Experience and Organizational Consequences of Blackberry Use," *Academy of Management Annual Meeting Proceeding* (2006), https://doi.org /10.5465/ambpp.2006.27169074.

39. Yue Lok (Francis) Cheung, Miu Chi (Vivian) Lun, and Hai-Jiang Wang, "Smartphone Use after Work Mediates the Link between Organizational Norm of Connectivity and Emotional Exhaustion: Will Workaholism Make a Difference?" *Stress and Health* 38, no. 1 (March 2020): 130–139, https://doi.org /10.1002/smi.3083.

40. Patrick M. Lencioni, "Make Your Values Mean Something," *Harvard Business Review*, July 2002, https://hbr.org/2002/07/make-your-values-mean -something.

41. *WeWork: Or the Making and Breaking of a $47 Billion Unicorn*, written and directed by Jed Rothstein, Hulu Original, 2021.

42. Anne Schaef and Diane Fassel, *The Addictive Organization: Why We Overwork, Cover Up, Pick Up the Pieces, Please the Boss, and Perpetuate Sick Organizations* (New York: HarperCollins, 1988), 125–126.

43. Schein and Schein, *Organizational Culture and Leadership*.

Chapter 5

1. Maev Kennedy, "Bank Intern Moritz Erhardt Died from Epileptic Seizure, Inquest Told," *Guardian*, November 22, 2013, https://www.theguardian .com/business/2013/nov/22/moritz-erhardt-merrill-lynch-intern-dead-inquest.

2. Justin McCurry, "Japanese Woman 'Dies from Overwork' After Logging 159 Hours of Overtime in a Month," *Guardian*, October 5, 2017, https://www .theguardian.com/world/2017/oct/05/japanese-woman-dies-overwork-159 -hours-overtime.

3. Ministry of Health, Labour and Welfare, 令和年度「過労死等の労災補償状況」を公表します(announcement of "Workers' Accident Compensation Status Such as Death from Overwork" in the first year of Reiwa), 2019, https://www.mhlw.go.jp/stf/newpage_11975.html; Max Schouw, "The Karōshi

Conundrum: Death by Overwork in Japan" (research paper #2140428, Avans School of International Studies, Breda, Netherlands, 2021).

4. Frank Pega et al., "Global, Regional, and National Burdens of Ischemic Heart Disease and Stroke Attributable to Exposure to Long Working Hours for 194 Countries, 2000–2016: A Systematic Analysis from the WHO/ILO Joint Estimates of the Work-Related Burden of Disease and Injury, *Environment International* 154 (September 2021), https://doi.org/10.1016/j.envint.2021.106595.

5. Manisha Thakor, *MoneyZen: The Secret to Finding Your "Enough"* (New York: Harper Business, 2023).

6. Rhitu Chatterjee and Carmel Wroth, "WHO Redefines Burnout as a 'Syndrome' Linked to Chronic Stress at Work," *Morning Edition*, WNPR, May 28, 2019, https://www.npr.org/sections/health-shots/2019/05/28/727637944/who-redefines-burnout-as-a-syndrome-linked-to-chronic-stress-at-work.

7. George Fink, "Stress: The Health Epidemic of the 21st Century," *Neuroscience*, Elsevier SciTech Connect, April 26, 2016, https://scitechconnect.elsevier.com/stress-health-epidemic-21st-century/.

8. Theresa Agovino, "To Have and to Hold," SHRM, February 23, 2019, https://www.shrm.org/hr-today/news/all-things-work/pages/to-have-and-to-hold.aspx.

9. Tim Levin, "Goldman Sachs Junior Bankers Describe 'Inhumane' Working Conditions Where They Don't Have Time to Eat or Shower in a Brutal Internal Survey," *Business Insider*, March 18, 2021, https://www.businessinsider.com/goldman-sachs-junior-bankers-inhumane-working-conditions-survey-2021-3.

10. Kalyeena Makortoff, "Goldman Sachs Junior Banker Speaks Out over '18-Hour Shifts and Low Pay,'" *Guardian*, March 24, 2021, https://www.theguardian.com/business/2021/mar/24/goldman-sachs-junior-bankers-rebel-over-18-hour-shifts-and-low-pay.

11. Britney Nguyen and Emmalyse Brownstein, "Goldman Sachs Junior Bankers Work 98 Hours a Week, a New Survey Says—Making the Equivalent of About $22 an Hour," *Business Insider*, December 3, 2022, https://www.businessinsider.com/goldman-sachs-junior-analysts-working-100-hours-week-survey-2022-12.

12. Kyle Lewis et al., *The Results Are In: The UK's Four-Day Week Pilot* (Crookham Village, Hampshire, UK: Autonomy, 2023), https://static1.squarespace.com/static/60b956cbe7bf6f2efd86b04e/t/63f3df56276b3e6d7870207e/1676926845047/UK-4-Day-Week-Pilot-Results-Report-2023.pdf.

13. Juliet B. Schor, *The Overworked American: The Unexpected Decline of Leisure* (New York: HarperCollins, 1992), 4.

14. David M. Maklan, *The Four-Day Workweek: Blue Collar Adjustment to Nonconventional Arrangement of Work and Leisure Time* (New York: Praeger Publishers, 1977).

15. "Four-Day Week 'an Overwhelming Success' in Iceland," BBC News, July 6, 2021, https://www.bbc.com/news/business-57724779; Peter Barck-Holst et al., "Reduced Working Hours and Stress in the Swedish Social Services:

A Longitudinal Study," *International Social Work* 60, no. 4 (2017): 897–913, https://doi.org/10.1177/0020872815580045; Timo Anttila and Jouko Nätti, "Experiments of Reduced Working Hours in Finnish Municipalities," *Journal of Human Resource Costing and Accounting* 4, no. 2 (1999): 45–61, https://doi .org/10.1108/eb029057.

16. Juliet B. Schor et al., *The Four Day Week: Assessing Global Trials of Reduced Work Time with No Reduction in Pay* (Auckland, NZ: Four Day Week Global, 2022), https://static1.squarespace.com/static/60b956cbe7bf6f2efd86b04e /t/6387be703530a824fc3adf58/1669840498593/.

17. Lewis et al., *The Results Are In.*

18. Kate Morgan, "Why Workers Just Won't Stop Quitting," BBC, August 18, 2022, https://www.bbc.com/worklife/article/20220817-why-workers-just-wont -stop-quitting; Andrea Hsu, "As the Pandemic Recedes, Millions of Workers Are Saying 'I Quit,'" NPR, June 24, 2021, https://www.npr.org/2021/06/24/1007914455 /as-the-pandemic-recedes-millions-of-workers-are-saying-i-quit.

19. Learn more about the implementation of STAR at a *Fortune* 500 firm in Erin L. Kelly and Phyllis Moen's *Overload: How Good Jobs Went Bad and What We Can Do About It* (Princeton, NJ: Princeton University Press, 2020).

20. Sarah Green Carmichael, "The Research Is Clear: Long Hours Backfire for People and Companies," hbr.org, August 19, 2015, https://hbr.org/2015/08 /the-research-is-clear-long-hours-backfire-for-people-and-for-companies.

21. For other resources related to organizational change management, Society for Human Resource Management (SHRM) members could check out the SHRM toolkit *Managing Organizational Change* (https://www.shrm.org /ResourcesAndTools/tools-and-samples/toolkits/Pages/default.aspx), and another recommendation is John Kotter's book *Accelerate* (Boston: Harvard Business Review Press, 2014).

22. For those interested in a readiness assessment specific to the implementation of a worker health and well-being initiative, I recommend checking out the Organizational Readiness Tool (ORT), which was developed specifically for the implementation of a participatory Total Worker Health program by researchers at the Center for the Promotion of Health in the New England Workplace: https://www.uml.edu/research/cph-new/healthy-work -participatory-program/get-ready/assess-readiness/readiness.aspx.

23. Leslie A. Perlow, *Sleeping with Your Smartphone: How to Break the 24-7 Habit and Change the Way You Work* (Boston: Harvard Business Review Press, 2012).

24. John Kotter, *Leading Change* (Boston: Harvard Business Review Press, 1996).

25. Perlow, *Sleeping with Your Smartphone.*

26. Andrew Barnes, *The 4 Day Week: How the Flexible Work Revolution Can Increase Productivity, Profitability and Well-Being, and Create a Sustainable Future* (London: Piatkus, 2020).

27. Barnes, *The 4 Day Week.*

28. Perlow, *Sleeping with Your Smartphone.*

29. Edgar H. Schein, *Organizational Culture and Leadership* (San Francisco: Jossey-Bass, 2004), 320.

30. Erin L. Kelly et al., "Gendered Challenge, Gendered Response: Confronting the Ideal Worker Norm in a White-Collar Organization," *Gender and Society* 24, no. 3 (2010): 281–303, https://doi.org/10.1177/0891243210372073.

31. Phyllis Moen, Erin Kelly, and Rachelle Hill, "Opting to Stay: Does a Worktime Control Intervention Reduce Turnover?" (paper presented at the Population Association of America meetings, Detroit, MI, 2009); Erin L. Kelly, Phyllis Moen, and Eric Tranby, "Control Over Work Time and Work-Family Conflict: Evidence from a Natural Experiment in a White-Collar Workplace" (paper presented at the Population Association of America meetings, Detroit, MI, 2009); Phyllis Moen et al., "Improving Employee Wellness: Does Increasing Control Over Work Time Matter?" (paper presented at the Eastern Sociological Society meetings, Boston, 2010).

32. John Hollon, "Goodbye ROWE: Best Buy Ends Flex Work Program It Was Famous For," *TNLT Newsletter*, March 6, 2013, https://www.tlnt.com/goodbye-rowe-best-buy-ends-flex-work-program-it-was-famous-for.

33. Cali Ressler and Jody Thompson, *Why Work Sucks and How to Fix It: No Schedules, No Meetings, No Joke—The Simple Change That Can Make Your Job Terrific* (New York: Portfolio, 2008).

34. Steven Kerr, "On the Folly of Rewarding A, While Hoping for B," *Academy of Management Executive* 9, no. 1 (February 1995): 7–14, https://www.jstor.org/stable/4165235.

35. Perlow, *Sleeping with Your Smartphone.*

36. William J. Becker et al., "Killing Me Softly: Organizational E-Mail Monitoring Expectations' Impact on Employee and Significant Other Well-Being," *Journal of Management* 47, no. 4 (2021): 1024–1052, https://doi.org/10.1177/0149206319890655.

37. Leslie A. Perlow and Jessica L. Porter, "Making Time Off Predictable and Required," *Harvard Business Review*, October 2009, 102–109.

38. Larissa K. Barber et al., "How Managers Can Reduce 'Always On' Work Stress in Teams: An Optimal Work Availability Framework," *Organizational Dynamics* 52, no. 3 (2023): 100992, https://doi.org/10.1016/j.orgdyn.2023.100992.

39. "Democratic Rate Plan Favored by Roosevelt [and other news]," *New York Times*, March 7, 1906, 3, https://www.nytimes.com/1906/03/07/archives/democratic-rate-plan-favored-by-roosevelt-bailey-has-proposed-a-new.html.

40. Frederick W. Taylor, *Scientific Management* (New York: Harper & Brothers, 1911). It should be noted that Taylor's practices have been (rightly) criticized for exploiting workers.

41. Emily M. Hunter and Cindy Wu, "Give Me a Better Break: Choosing Workday Break Activities to Maximize Resource Recovery," *Journal of Applied*

Psychology 101, no. 2 (February 2016): 302–311, http://dx.doi.org/10.1037 /apl0000045.

42. Stephanie Mertens et al., "The Effectiveness of Nudging: A Meta-Analysis of Choice Architecture Interventions Across Behavioral Domains," *PNAS* 119, no. 1 (December 30, 2022), https://www.pnas.org/doi/pdf/10.1073 /pnas.2107346118.

43. Elizabeth Velema, "Nudging and Social Marketing Techniques Encourage Employees to Make Healthier Food Choices: A Randomized Controlled Trial in 30 Worksite Cafeterias in the Netherlands," *American Journal of Clinical Nutrition* 107 (2018): 236–246, https://doi.org/10.1093/ajcn/nqx045.

44. Literature on social distance includes work by Adam D. Galinsky, "Power Reduces the Press of the Situation: Implications for Creativity, Conformity, and Dissonance," *Journal of Personality and Social Psychology* 95, no.6 (2008): 1450–1466, https://doi.org/10.1037/a0012633; Joe C. Magee, "Power and Social Distance," *Current Opinion in Psychology* 33 (2020): 33–37, https://doi .org/10.1016/j.copsyc.2019.06.005; and Rachel E. Sturm and John Antonakis, "Interpersonal Power: A Review, Critique, and Research Agenda," *Journal of Management* 41, no. 1 (2015): 136–163, https://doi.org/10.1177/0149206314555769.

45. Qikun Niu, "Exploring the Nomological Net of Micro-Breaks from a Cross-level Perspective" (Phd diss., George Mason University, 2016).

46. "Billionaire Buffett and the Only Banker He Trusts," *Evening Standard*, September 25, 2008, https://www.standard.co.uk/hp/front/billionaire-buffett -and-the-only-banker-he-trusts-6813262.html.

47. Dan Kadlec, "Buffett's New Message: Damn the Deal, Keep Work and Life in Balance," *Time*, May 25, 2012, https://business.time.com/2012/05/25 /buffetts-new-message-damn-the-deal-keep-work-and-life-in-balance/.

48. Bryson Kearl, "5 Reasons We Offer Paid Paid Vacation," *Bamboo HR* (blog), June 16, 2016, https://www.bamboohr.com/blog/5-reasons-offer-paid -paid-vacation-love.

49. Anna Baluch, "Average PTO in the US and Other PTO Statistics (2023)," *Forbes*, March 30, 2023, https://www.forbes.com/advisor/business/pto-statistics.

50. Perlow and Porter, "Making Time Off Predictable and Required."

51. These suggestions are backed by the theoretical framework of job-demands -control model proposed by Robert Karasek Jr., "Job Demands, Job Decision Latitude, and Mental Strain: Implications for Job Redesign," *Administrative Science Quarterly* 24, no. 2 (1979): 285–308, https://www.jstor.org/stable/2392498.

Conclusion

1. Cristian Balducci et al., "A Within-Individual Investigation on the Relationship between Day Level Workaholism and Systolic Blood Pressure," *Work and Stress* 36, no. 4 (2022): 337–354, https://doi.org/10.1080/02678373.2 021.1976883; Lieke L. ten Brummelhuis, Nancy P. Rothbard, and Benjamin Uhrich, "Beyond Nine to Five: Is Working to Excess Bad for Health?" *Academy of*

Management Discoveries 3, no. 3 (2017): 262–283, https://doi.org/10.5465/amd
.2015.0115; Damiano Girardi et al., "Is Workaholism Associated with
Inflammatory Response? The Moderating Role of Work Engagement," *TPM-
Testing, Psychometrics, Methodology in Applied Psychology* 26, no. 2 (2019): 305–322,
https://doi.org/10.4473/TPM26.2.9; Marisa Salanova et al., "Your Work May Be
Killing You! Workaholism, Sleep Problems and Cardiovascular Risk," *Work and
Stress* 30, no. 3 (2016): 228–242, https://doi.org/10.1080/02678373.2016.1203373.

2. This idea comes from my conversations with Dr. Larissa Barber and also
her 2020 presentation "From 'Always On' to 'Optimally On': Managing Online
Availability Expectations in Telework" at the NORA Services Sector Council
Webinar.

3. Sandy K. Piderit, "Rethinking Resistance and Recognizing Ambivalence:
A Multidimensional View of Attitudes Toward an Organizational Change,"
Academy of Management Review 25, no. 4 (2000): 783–794, https://doi.org/10.2307
/259206.

4. Joan C. Williams, "The Pandemic Has Exposed the Fallacy of the 'Ideal
Worker,'" hbr.org, May 10, 2020, https://hbr.org/2020/05/the-pandemic-has
-exposed-the-fallacy-of-the-ideal-worker.

INDEX

ACKNOWLEDGMENTS

This book wouldn't have been possible without an entire community of supporters. I want to first highlight two individuals who played a pivotal role in this process. First, an enormous thank you to Brigid Schulte. Brigid, I am so grateful that we connected through your podcast and that we've kept in touch ever since. Thank you for being so generous with your time and for your excellent advice, encouragement, and guidance as I was entertaining the idea of publishing a book. I am forever grateful for everything I've learned from you, and a huge thank you for being willing to make the introductions that ultimately led me to the second key individual I'd like to acknowledge—my editor at Harvard Business Review Press, Scott Berinato. Scott was a champion of this book from day one, and I am honored that he saw enough promise in my proposal to work with a first-time author. Scott helped turn my academic-style writing into something much more digestible and relatable, and he was also a constant source of encouragement whenever I felt the pressure of a looming deadline. His creativity and vision elevated the book to a level that I could not have accomplished on my own, and I have him to thank for the book's catchy title. And most importantly, he believed in the book and in me.

The entire team at Harvard Business Review Press has been amazing. In addition to Scott, I'd like to thank the many individuals who helped with various aspects of the publishing process: production editors Anne Starr and Jen Waring, your skills are unmatched, and I am so appreciative of the time, attention, and level of detail you applied to the making of this book. Thanks to editorial coordinator Cheyenne Paterson and to the marketing and communications team at the Press: Julie Devoll, Alexandra Kephart, Felicia Sinusas, Jon Shipley, Jordan Concannon, Lindsey Dietrich, and Sally Ashworth. I am so grateful to have so many talented individuals steering me through this process.

I am grateful to the professors who taught me all about industrial-organizational psychology during my doctoral training at Wayne State University: Boris Baltes, Christopher Berry, Marcus Dickson, Sebastiano Fisicaro, James LeBreton, and Cary Lichtman. Thanks for taking a chance on an applicant who had never worked in a research lab prior to graduate school. I learned so much during my time at WSU, and I hope that I can create a similar impact on my own students. To my colleagues and friends, both at the University of Georgia (UGA) and beyond, you have been such a fantastic support network throughout this process. In particular, thank you to my friend and colleague Michelle VanDellen for providing much-needed words of encouragement during our many writing sessions at Panera.

A special thanks to Workaholics Anonymous for its willingness to share information about my project with its members. To each and every person who volunteered to speak with me and my team about how workaholism and overwork have affected their lives, thank you so much for sharing your stories. Thanks also to the following workplace experts, professors, and industry leaders for their invaluable insights on the topic: Emily Ballesteros, Larissa Barber, Andrew Barnes, Lauren Broyles, Steven Currall, Marnie Dobson, Dr. Darria Gillespie, Adam Grant, Lauren Kuykendall,

Chris Lovato, Melissa Mazmanian, Alex Soojung-Kim Pang, Brigid Schulte, and Manisha Thakor. Speaking with each of you was one of the most fulfilling parts of this entire process. Finally, many thanks to my research assistants, who helped interview the spouses of workaholics, transcribed each of the interviews, and assisted with various other tasks for the book.

Thank you to my family for your support and encouragement along the way. Dad, even though you were not here to celebrate the joy of learning your daughter was going to be a published author of a book, I know you would have insisted you receive the first signed copy, and you would have proudly displayed this book on your bookshelf. Thanks for always encouraging me to think positively. I do my best to follow your advice. Alex and Evan, thanks for being so patient with me over the past year as I put in extra hours to write this book. And Kurt, thank you for shouldering the bulk of the household tasks during my busy times and for your constant support and encouragement. I love you all very much.

Last, but certainly not least, I'd like to acknowledge one person who is no longer with us. When I was halfway through writing this book, one of our beloveds I-O graduate students, Beth Buchanan, was tragically killed in a car accident. Beth was one of those people who made a profound and lasting impression on everyone who crossed her path. She was brilliant, witty, thoughtful, kind, and passionate about helping others through her research and service to the community. Beth, you will always be a treasured part of our I-O family, and we miss you very much. And to everyone who has read this far (thank you, by the way!), it would mean so much to Beth's family if you took the time to learn more about Beth's life and legacy by visiting bethebuchanan.org.

ABOUT THE AUTHOR

MALISSA CLARK is an associate professor of industrial-organizational (I-O) psychology at the University of Georgia, where she has been on the faculty since 2013. Currently, Clark serves as Associate Head of the Department of Psychology and Director of the Healthy Work Lab. She is a recognized expert on the topics of workaholism, overwork, burnout, and employee well-being.

Clark earned her PhD in I-O psychology from Wayne State University and her BA in organizational studies from the University of Michigan. She has received awards for her writing and mentoring, and her work has been funded by the National Institute for Occupational Safety and Health (NIOSH) and the Society for Industrial and Organizational Psychology (SIOP). In 2023 Clark was named a fellow of SIOP, a status that recognizes unusual and outstanding contributions that have an important impact on I-O psychology.

Clark's work has been published in premier outlets such as the *Journal of Applied Psychology*, the *Journal of Management*, and the *Journal of Organizational Behavior*. She serves on the editorial boards of the *Journal of Applied Psychology* and *Personnel Psychology* and as action editor for the *Journal of Business and Psychology* and *Occupational Health Science*. Clark is passionate about bridging the scientist-practitioner gap and advocating for healthier workplaces and worker well-being through her speaking and consulting. Her work has been featured on various podcasts and in outlets such as *Time*, *US News and World Report*, the *New York Times*, and *The Atlantic*. She currently serves as a member of the NIOSH Healthy Work Design and Well-Being Council. When not working, she enjoys spending time with her family and traveling.